Passing the **National Admissions Test** for **Law**

Third edition

Passing the **National Admissions Test** for **Law**

Rosalie Hutton, Glenn Hutton and Fraser Sampson

Third edition

LearningMatters

First published in 2005 by Law Matters Ltd
Reprinted in 2006
Reprinted in 2007 (twice)
Second edition published in 2008 by Learning Matters Ltd
Reprinted in 2008
Reprinted in 2009
Reprinted in 2010
Third edition published in 2011

© 2011 Rosalie Hutton, Glenn Hutton and Fraser Sampson

British Library Cataloguing in Publication Data
A CIP record for this book is available from the British Library

ISBN: 978 0 85725 485 6

This book is available in the following ebook formats:
Adobe ebook ISBN: 978 0 85725 487 0
EPUB ebook ISBN: 978 0 85725 486 3
Kindle ISBN: 978 0 85725 488 7

The right of Rosalie Hutton, Glenn Hutton and Fraser Sampson to be identified
as the Authors of this work has been asserted by them in accordance with the
Copyright, Designs and Patents Act 1988.

® LNAT is a registered mark of the LNAT Consortium Ltd

Cover design by Toucan
Project Management by Deer Park Productions, Tavistock
Typeset by Pantek Arts Ltd, Maidstone, Kent
Print and bound in Great Britain by Bell & Bain Ltd, Glasgow

Learning Matters Ltd
20 Cathedral Yard
Exeter   .
EX1 1HB
01392 215560
info@learningmatters.co.uk
www.learningmatters.co.uk

Mixed Sources
Product group from well-managed
forests and other controlled sources
www.fsc.org Cert no. TT-COC-002769
© 1996 Forest Stewardship Council
FSC

Contents

Preface

This book resulted from a decision by several leading UK universities to introduce an assessment for people applying to read for undergraduate law degrees. The demand for these courses has far outweighed availability and the universities determined the need for a vehicle which would better identify applicants with an aptitude for success in law. Since the original concept of further assessment was formed other universities have followed suit and it is anticipated that more universities will require such assessment over time.

The purpose of this book is essentially to provide a step-by-step guide to understanding verbal reasoning tests and the production of a well-reasoned essay.

This is the third edition of the book and it has been updated to include information about the university application process for prospective law undergraduates. Since the last edition the examining body has increased the number of passages and questions in the test. More significantly the style, and to some extent the complexity, of the text passages has also been developed. The practice test and answers contained in Part III of the book have been completely replaced to reflect these developments.

Rosalie Hutton is an Occupational Psychologist, specialising in the field of assessment and testing, who designs and publishes a range of psychological assessment measures. Critical reasoning tests have been used commercially for a number of years in the recruitment and selection of staff and Rosalie provides the rationale for the use of these tests together with a developmental approach to understanding critical reasoning type questions and how best to arrive at the correct answer.

Glenn Hutton and Fraser Sampson have both worked at a senior level in a major assessment organisation which has tested several thousand people a year using multiple-choice type questions. During this time they had close links with the National Board of Medical Examiners in the United States which tests up to 100,000 doctors a year using online multiple-choice tests. They are also technical authors for Oxford University Press annually producing manuals associated with the criminal law. Fraser is currently the Chief Executive and Solicitor for West Yorkshire Police Authority.

Part I
Introduction

1. The National Admissions Test for Law (LNAT®)

The level of competition for places on some university law courses is extremely fierce. As a means of filtering applicants, even those with A grades, a number of universities require they sit a standardised admissions test called the National Admissions Test for Law (LNAT®).

The LNAT® is an on-screen test with two sections.

Section A has changed for the 2010–11 testing year increasing the number of passages from ten to 12, questions from 30 to 42, and the time from 80 to 95 minutes. This section is designed to assess a candidate's ability to read, understand, analyse and make logical deductions from passages of text in formal English. The test is designed to be an assessment of 'the verbal reasoning skills at the heart of legal education' and does not require any knowledge of the law.

Section B requires that a candidate can write a reasoned and substantiated argument that justifies their response to one of the five questions provided. The time allowed for the essay is 40 minutes and it should be about 500–600 words in length, and at the most 750 words. The test is designed to be an assessment of fundamental intellectual skills and as with **Section A** requires no prior knowledge of the law.

The LNAT® is set by Pearson Assessments and Testing in conjunction with Edexcel. Pearson is also responsible for marking the multiple-choice element of the test. Each law school operates a slightly different admissions policy and so each one will use the free essay component in a slightly different way. Some may refer to it, for example, throughout a student's interview. Others will compare it against a student's personal statement on the UCAS form. The essay may also be used as a means of distinguishing between borderline candidates when the A-level results are announced. The setting and administration of the test is overseen by LNAT® Consortium Ltd, a company jointly owned by the participating universities.

Because of these variations in the way in which the test results will be used, there is no fixed weight or 'pass mark' to the LNAT®. This may seem slightly odd, particularly for those students who have just spent the last five years of their education being assessed against nationally agreed pass/fail criteria. However, just because there is no pass mark it does not mean that the LNAT® is easy or irrelevant. The LNAT® results and A-levels (or equivalent qualifications), along with AS-levels and GCSEs, will be assessed in combination with other elements. These may include the personal statement and reference from the UCAS form and, in certain cases, performance at interview. Therefore the LNAT® forms an important element in the overall criteria against which applications will be judged.

As well as taking the LNAT®, you need to apply for your chosen course in the normal way. Undertaking the LNAT® does not constitute an application to any university. The LNAT® is sat at a test centre near your home, school or college; there are about 150 test centres in the UK with the network extending to other places in the world including Singapore, Prague, Toronto, Buenos Aires and three centres in China. A current fee of £50 is charged for sitting the LNAT® at UK/EU test centres and £70 at test centres outside the UK/EU.

More detailed information and 'frequently asked questions' can be obtained from the LNAT® website at **www.lnat.ac.uk**.

The universities/courses currently requiring applicants to sit the LNAT® are listed below:

University of Birmingham:	M100, MR11, MR12, M1N1
University of Bristol:	M100, MR11, MR12
University of Durham:	M101, M102
University of Glasgow:	M114, M1R7, M1R1, M121, M1R2, M122, M1R3, M1M9, M1RR, M1R4, M123, MN11, MN12, MV13, ML11, MQ13, MQ15, ML17, MV11, MV15, ML12, MR17
Kings College London:	M100, M121
University of Leeds:	M100, MR11, MN14, MN12
University of Nottingham:	M100, M101, M1R1, M1R2
University of Oxford:	M100, M101, M102, M141, M142, M144, M145, M146
University College London:	M100, M101, M102, M141, M142, M143, M144, M145, M146

The following non-UK universities may also require the LNAT®:

NUI Maynooth:	MH115, MH406 and MH119 (mature entry only)
IE University (choice of tests applies)	

2. How will this book help me?

This book has been produced to provide any person preparing for the National Admissions Test for Law (LNAT®) with an in-depth understanding of both Parts A and B of the Test.

Part I of the book examines your choice of a career in law and the admissions process to university. The process outlined is simply a summary and is not intended to replace the UCAS Progression Series publication Law: For entry to university and college. The UCAS book is really a must for any applicant, providing not just details about admissions but all the law courses available at UK universities.

Part II provides a clear explanation of the rationale, development and use of verbal reasoning tests. It also examines the style and format of the multiple-choice questions used in the LNAT® and how best to approach these. Finally, this part provides a step-by-step, developmental approach to answering verbal reasoning questions. By the end of this part you should have a good understanding of verbal reasoning type questions and how best to arrive at the correct answer.

Part III replicates Section A of the LNAT®. In the actual test candidates are allowed 95 minutes and you might consider using the practice test to time yourself against this constraint for some indication as to your level of performance. Bear in mind that the on-screen test will have the passage of text and questions on the same screen whereas with the book when answering questions you will need to keep turning back to the page containing the passage; inevitably this will increase your time by several minutes overall. This practice test has not been written to be time constrained but as a vehicle: (a) to consolidate what has been learnt from the previous part; and (b) to give you the confidence when dealing with such questions. Rather than simply giving the 'correct response', the answers to the practice test provide the rationale for both the correct and incorrect answers. This approach has been proved to be effective in developing a person's knowledge and understanding of a particular subject.

The excellent LNAT® website gives candidates the opportunity to take two on-screen practice tests and you are strongly advised to complete these. Although a separate file provides a scoring template to check whether your answer is correct or not, there is no rationale for either correct or incorrect answers. Although the answer might often be 'obvious' there are occasions where a more detailed explanation would be beneficial.

Finally, Part IV looks at essay writing skills. This is not meant to be an exhaustive review of these skills but does include essay style and structure, the use of critical thinking skills and the use of grammar and punctuation to enable you to write a well-reasoned essay.

In addition to the practice tests and information given here, there are other things that can be done to prepare for reading law at degree level. While it may seem very informal, one of the most effective ways both to prepare for and succeed in studying law and jurisprudence is to read a 'quality' newspaper. In fact the LNAT® Consortium recommends this.

This book does not claim to be able to help you do well in the test but it should speed up your reactions and give you confidence in the style of questions you will encounter. GOOD LUCK!

3. Application to read law

For an undergraduate law degree you are required to apply online to both UCAS (**www.ucas.com**) and LNAT® (**www.lnat.ac.uk**) following the general time-table below:

August: LNAT® registration begins.
September: UCAS applications and LNAT® test sittings commence.
January: Submit UCAS forms and end of LNAT® test sittings.
June: Final closing date for late applications and those outside the UK.

Note that for the University of Oxford, LNAT® registration is required by October and the LNAT® to be sat by November.

Exact dates, details about choices, clearing and deferred entry are available on the UCAS website.

Deciding if law is really for you

You should already realise that training to become a solicitor or barrister demands a considerable commitment over a number of years. For example, once you decide to become a solicitor, it will take at least three years to train if you are a law graduate. However, if you are a non-law graduate it takes at least four years, and at least six years if you are not a graduate. This is just a reminder then that qualifying as a solicitor or barrister is not easy; you will have the intellectual challenge of exams, and you will need to fund your own studies.

According to the Law Society, the representative body for solicitors in England and Wales, a career as a solicitor will demand several qualities of you:

- intellectual ability – law is a complex entity
- versatility – no two days will be the same
- a desire to work with and for people
- commitment – training to become a solicitor is rigorous, requiring substantial effort and resources.

Exam results

Increasing competition for places at law school now demands a common entry requirement of AAB at A-level. There is no specific requirement in relation to the subjects at A-level but comments by the Russell Group suggest that member universities will favour traditional subjects (or at least two such subjects). English, history and economics are a good example of relevant subjects as to an extent they reflect some of the rigour and skills found in studying law. Although an A-level in law is not a pre-requisite, this obviously evidences an interest in the subject and is looked on favourably by universities.

Finding out about life in the law

The Law Society and Law Careers Advice Network (LCAN) are probably the two better known organisations providing law career details and both have useful information available on their websites. Another useful website is that of the Solicitors Regulation Authority and in particular the section headed *Student membership and completion of the academic stage of training*. This section also includes a subsection *Your character and suitability to be a solicitor* – this may be worth a read. For example, if you have been convicted of armed robbery you may want to reconsider whether a career in law is your best option!

Deciding on a university

There are currently over 100 universities offering degrees in law. However, you need to find the university (or college) which best suits your needs in relation to the specific areas covered, the actual course content and the teaching methods employed. All of these are important to ensure you have the best opportunity of achieving your full potential. It will be worth spending time with this. Obviously, you should also remember that only nine UK universities currently use the LNAT® in their application process.

Make sure the degree you are applying for is a qualifying LLB (Bachelor of Law) degree. Some universities offer BAs (Bachelor of Arts) in law. But unlike the LLB, some of these courses may not be counted as one of the steps towards qualifying as a lawyer, as they do not cover all seven foundations of legal knowledge, namely: criminal law; equity and trusts; EU law; contract law; tort law; property law; and public law (including constitutional law, administrative law and human rights law). The Solicitors Regulation Authority website (**www.sra.org.uk**) keeps a list of all qualifying law degrees and the universities that offer them.

It is interesting to note that although commercial law firms make a big deal of their willingness to recruit students from any university, the fact remains that, at least for the time being, the majority of trainees still hail from older universities, so take this into account when choosing a university.

Writing your personal statement

Before offering a place, universities are looking at three main things: your exam results, your referee's statement and your personal statement. Exam results and referees' statements seldom help universities to make selection decisions, whereas the personal statement is your opportunity to convince the university to offer you a place. They want to see that you will fit into university life, not just academically but socially as well. Apart from telling the reader of your personal statement why you want to read law you should also include information about your work experience, volunteer work, academic commitment and extracurricular activities.

Work experience can often be difficult for those of you who are coming straight from full-time education but access schemes at weekends and during holidays are often available, especially in the final year of A-levels. If you have a family member or friend working in the legal profession then they may be able to arrange a placement, or your school or college may have a placement scheme with local law firms. However, do not be dismayed if you have problems gaining work experience; universities are aware of how difficult this can be.

Volunteer work is considered by many as important in the sense that it demonstrates a commitment to helping others in the community and develops your people and softer skills. Getting involved is easy and you should look for something you would enjoy and that you might stick at for months or longer. Lots of volunteering positions only require up to four hours' commitment a week and with some there are opportunities to attend training courses, e.g. first aid. Careers advisers may be able to help organise volunteer work or you can visit the following websites: **www.volunteering.org.uk** (this is the Volunteering England site and contains information and addresses); **www.do-it.org.uk** (this is 'volunteering made easy' – just enter your address and the type of project you want to get involved with). So if you aren't volunteering you might consider it's time to get off your backside and start to help others – oh and by the way, it can be FUN and it's FREE!

Academic commitment means demonstrating that you understand the commitment required for the hard work you will face to complete your degree and beyond. Your exam results do not amply demonstrate your commitment to studying but reading up on an area of law that might interest you would do – so make a note of everything you read outside your A-level course work in preparation for completing the personal statement.

Extracurricular activities are important as these provide evidence that you are a well-rounded person with a number of hobbies and interests. This may include playing representative sport, being a member of a society, being a musician or undertaking the Duke of Edinburgh Awards scheme. Where possible evidence of positions of responsibility is beneficial to demonstrate your leadership skills and the fact that you are confident and willing to undertake such responsibilities.

The importance of the personal statement cannot be overemphasised. You need to start it early in the application process and ensure it is providing the best impression of yourself, your skills and your ambitions. No doubt you will not be completely alone in preparing the statement as teachers and tutors take considerable interest in its preparation.

Interviews

First of all, not all universities use interviews; some interview as a matter of process, while others only interview where clarification of the application may be required. Assuming you are called for interview you will undoubtedly be required to demonstrate the following:

- academic ability
- capacity to deal with the rigours of the course
- commitment to a career in law
- logic and reasoning ability
- knowledge of current affairs, especially those concerning the law.

These areas are really what you would expect and the last point reiterates the benefits of regularly reading a 'quality' newspaper.

Part II
Verbal Reasoning Tests

4. Verbal reasoning

Verbal reasoning has been one of the cornerstones of aptitude testing since it first became fashionable over sixty years ago. Although still essentially 'verbal' reasoning tests, where the test is of a far more complex and intellectual nature, these are more commonly referred to as 'critical reasoning' tests. Undoubtedly, given the LNAT® definition of their 'verbal reasoning test' (comprehension, interpretation, analysis, synthesis, induction and deduction) Section A of the LNAT® fits within the meaning of 'critical reasoning'. Therefore, for the purposes of this part of the book the LNAT® test will be construed as a critical reasoning test.

Critical reasoning, also known as critical thinking, is fundamentally concerned with the way arguments are structured and produced by whatever media; discussion, debate, a paper, a report, an article or an essay. The following are the generally accepted criteria for critical thinking:

- the ability to differentiate between facts and opinions
- the ability to examine assumptions
- being open minded as you search for explanations, causes and solutions
- being aware of valid or invalid argument forms
- staying focussed on the whole picture, while examining the specifics
- verifying sources
- deducing and judging inductions
- inducing and judging inductions
- making value judgements
- defining terms and judging definitions
- deciding on actions
- being objective
- a willingness and ability always to look at alternatives.

The above list is not meant to be an exhaustive list of all the criteria of critical thinking but it provides an overview of some of the basic principles that underpin the LNAT®.

Applying your own critical reasoning, you will realise at this point that some of the criteria listed will lend themselves more readily to the LNAT® multiple-choice questions while others will be more relevant to the essay section. A further discussion on critical thinking is contained in Part IV.

The fact that universities are now looking at setting aptitude tests (such as the LNAT®) which involve critical thinking reflects the recognition that critical thinking is now being promoted in education generally. There is now an AS-level course (offered by the OCR Examination Board) in critical thinking. The course has five major areas: identifying the elements of reasoning; evaluating reasoning; recognising and evaluating assumptions; clarifying expressions and ideas; presenting a reasoned case in a clear, logical and coherent way. The assessment for this AS-level is by examination; there is no course work element and the examination is of similar format to the LNAT®, i.e. questions related to passages and essays.

In the commercial field, professional psychometric testing has for many years employed critical reasoning tests for similar reasons, i.e. the need for organisations to recruit the right people, with the right skills etc. In today's economic climate competition for jobs and training is intense and all the applicants find themselves in a selection pool of similarly qualified people, presenting a problem, not only for the applicant, but also for those who have a limited number of training places or job vacancies to offer. This makes the selection process difficult – from both perspectives. Therefore, the psychometrics profession, which comprises mainly test developers and publishers, has grown into a multi-million-pound industry. Test developers are usually psychologists who specialise in testing (psychometrists) and it is usually their remit to construct tests of aptitude such as verbal, numerical, spatial ability etc., as well as tests of other characteristics, such as personality.

When making selection decisions – whether they are for training, further education or for job appointments – the area of critical thinking/reasoning is deemed to be very important. This is largely because these skills are important in performing the roles themselves, particularly those in management. Graduate/managerial level aptitude tests of verbal reasoning, which are basically assessing the understanding of words, grammar, spelling, word relationships etc., may provide an objective assessment of a candidate's verbal ability. However, these types of test are seen by some to lack face validity (that is, they do not appear to be job related) when used for graduate/managerial roles. People of this level often object to being given 'IQ tests' and prefer an assessment that appears to replicate, to some extent, the content of the job, i.e. critically evaluating reports. It is also believed by some that classic verbal reasoning tests do not provide an indication of an individual's ability to think critically, therefore psychometrists have developed what are generally called critical reasoning tests, which are similar in format to the LNAT® and are described in the following section.

5. Format and design of multiple-choice questions

Introduction

This section provides a brief overview of multiple-choice question tests and then examines their format and design and in particular that being used for the LNAT®.

Which of the following are true of multiple-choice tests and questions?

A   The tests are very simplistic

B   The questions are easy to answer

C   The tests are a poor substitute for real examinations

D   A good guessing strategy will always get you a decent mark

The answer, of course, is none of the above.

Multiple-choice tests have a very good track record in the field of assessment and particularly in selection. Multiple-choice questions are a technique which simply tests the candidates' knowledge and understanding of a particular subject on the date of the test. They make candidates read and think but not write about the question set, as in the case with essay-type questions.

It is true that there have been a number of long-held criticisms – and myths – about multiple-choice tests. For one, it has long been a criticism of multiple-choice questions that they are too simple-minded and trivial. What this observation really means is that it is perfectly obvious to the candidate what they have to do. There are no marks for working out what the examiner wants – it's obvious. But this is not the same as saying that the answer is obvious; far from it. In addition, multiple-choice questions are often referred to by students as being 'multiple guess' questions, on the basis that the right answer lies in one of the options given and therefore you have a good mathematical chance of happening upon the right answer. Although systematic and even completely random guessing does occur in multiple-choice tests, their effects can be minimised and their use identified by properly constructed, presented and timed tests. The people who design and analyse multiple-choice tests are often just as interested in what wrong answers you give as the right ones. This is because, apart from other things, patterns can be discerned and compared with others taking the same test and tendencies towards certain answers (e.g. always choosing option B) will stand out.

In short, guessing is easy to spot and unlikely to succeed. Given that the purpose of the LNAT® is to inform the overall decision-making process in selecting you over your fellow applicants (rather than simply achieving a bad result or score) relying on guesswork is a poor strategy.

Multiple-choice tests are used extensively both in Europe and the United States, from staged tests in schools through to university selection and assessment, to some of the most complex and high stake professional trade qualifications.

The strength of these tests is that they can provide fair and objective testing on a huge scale at small cost, in the sense that their administration is standardised and their developers can demonstrate that the results are not going to vary according to the marker, a criticism of essay type question tests.

The format and design of the multiple-choice questions used for the LNAT® follows the general educational model.

The following descriptions of the format and design of multiple-choice questions has been informed by two publications. Firstly, *Assessment & Testing: A survey of research*; University of Cambridge Local Examinations Syndicate (1995). The University of Cambridge Local Examinations Syndicate has been in existence for over 130 years and prepares examinations for over 100 countries. Secondly, *Constructing Written Test Questions For the Basic Clinical Sciences* (Second Edition, Susan M Case and David B Swanson, National Board of Medical Examiners (1998)). The National Board of Medical Examiners, which is based in the USA, uses multiple-choice questions to test in excess of 100,000 medical students each year including foreign doctors, at numerous sites throughout the world.

In all, multiple-choice testing properly conducted is well established, well respected and well used across the professional assessment world.

Format of multiple-choice questions

There are a number of different formats that can be used for multiple-choice tests but at the present time the LNAT® uses only one such format; this is taken from the 'One Best Answer' family.

The 'One Best Answer' family, also known as A-type questions, are the most widely used in multiple-choice tests. They make explicit the number of choices to be selected and usually consist of a stem, a lead-in-question, followed by a series of choices. The LNAT® has determined a series of five choices.

Stem

The stem is usually a set of circumstances that can be presented in a number of different ways. The circumstances may be presented in a few simple sentences, as a document, a letter, some form of pictorial display or may be longer passages (as in the LNAT®), i.e. newspaper articles, extracts from books or periodicals. It provides all the information for the question that will follow.

For example a typical stem, for a question in the LNAT®, could be:

Consider the following argument.

'Research has shown that in the UK hundreds of thousands of people smoke cannabis and that the majority of these can otherwise be regarded as "law abiding citizens". They are rational people who know what they are doing. The reasons for using cannabis can be many but in the main its use is seen as a relaxant and no better or worse than smoking tobacco. There is also a growing number of people who use cannabis for health reasons to relieve the symptoms of their illness, for example, those suffering from severe arthritis. Medical opinion on this has generally agreed that the benefits to pain reduction are tangible. In the majority of other European countries cannabis for personal use is lawful so why do we continue to criminalise it?'

Lead-in question

The lead-in question identifies the exact answer the examiner requires from the circumstances provided in the stem.

For example, a typical lead-in question for the stem example given above could be:

Which of the following is an unarticulated assumption of the argument?

Five choices

The five choices provided will always consist of ONE correct answer and FOUR incorrect answers; these incorrect answers are often referred to as 'distracters'.

For example, typical choices for the stem and lead-in question example given above could be:

(a) The majority of people who smoke cannabis are rational people

(b) That cannabis relieves the pain of arthritis sufferers

(c) That people in the UK who use cannabis are criminals but in most of Europe they are not

(d) That the medical profession agree with the use of cannabis for certain complaints

(e) That smoking tobacco is as harmful to health as smoking cannabis

Answer and rationale

The question asks which of the choices is an unarticulated assumption of the argument? In other words, which is an unstated supposition as opposed to an explicit statement.

(a) That the majority of people who smoke cannabis are rational people

This is made explicit by reading the second and third sentences of the passage together and is therefore an incorrect answer choice.

(b) That cannabis relieves the pain of arthritis sufferers

This is directly stated in the passage in the fifth sentence of the passage and is therefore an incorrect answer choice.

(c) That people in the UK who use cannabis are criminals but in most of Europe they are not

The final sentence of the passage explicitly states, 'In the majority of other European countries cannabis for personal use is lawful…' and is therefore an incorrect answer choice.

(d) That the medical profession agree with the use of cannabis for certain complaints

The passage states that 'Medical opinion on this has generally agreed that the benefits to pain reduction are tangible', therefore, this is an unarticulated assumption of the author and is the correct answer choice.

(e) That smoking tobacco is as harmful to health as smoking cannabis

This cannot be assumed from the passage. In the passage it states '…its use is seen as a relaxant and no better or worse than smoking tobacco'. This has no relevance to 'health' issues and therefore this statement is an incorrect answer choice.

6. Approach to multiple-choice questions

Whatever the purpose or the design of the test, it is worth bearing in mind some general rules to follow when answering multiple-choice questions. Clearly, your score should be higher if you attempt to answer all of the questions in the test and avoid wild guessing. The average time for each passage and set of questions in the LNAT® is 8 minutes and you should plan not to spend any longer than this on any one passage. However, if you are running out of time you may attempt some 'educated' guesses but with 5 options available this may prove difficult. If there are questions you are unsure of you can place a mark against them for reviewing later.

Although it is often repeated at every level of testing and assessment in every walk of life, it is nevertheless worth reiterating – **always read the questions carefully**. It may help to read them more than once to avoid misreading a critical word(s) (e.g. reading 'inferred' instead of 'not inferred'). Given the focus on verbal reasoning in the LNAT® (and in the practical application of law generally) careful reading of the words presented is crucial.

Where all the options, or some of the options, begin with the same word(s), or appear very similar, be sure to mark the correct option.

When undertaking a multiple-choice test such as the LNAT® there are essentially two strategies that can be adopted.

Strategy 1

Carefully read the passage, then read each question and then go on to examine each of the options in turn to see whether it is possibly correct or whether it can be eliminated. This process of elimination should leave you with the correct answer. However, you should be aware that you might become more susceptible to the distracters and immediately believe one to be the correct answer. You may then go through a process of 'justifying' your choice to yourself and therefore not have an open mind to conflicting arguments elsewhere in the passage.

This strategy is the more conventional approach that would probably be followed by most test takers.

Strategy 2

Carefully read the passage and then attempt each question without looking at the options available. When you have arrived at a possible answer for the question you can examine the options to see if your choice, or a close match, is available. This process would validate or invalidate your answer thus allowing you to move on or review your answer.

Alternatively, you may read the question first and then carefully read the passage in an attempt to arrive at a possible answer before looking at the options.

This is a more deliberate strategy and feels less 'intuitive' than the first strategy above.

It is of course a matter of personal choice which of the two strategies you adopt. However, in either case, because the passages used in the test are fairly lengthy an initial skim read might be beneficial.

When reading the passages in the LNAT® it is important to examine closely the construction of the writers' arguments. How does the writer logically progress their argument? Notice how each stage of their argument is related overall, including the purposes of any examples or analogies.

Do not use your own knowledge of the subject matter to influence your answers even if your knowledge contradicts that of the author. As stated earlier, the concept of these tests is not to test individual prior knowledge – it is to present everyone competing against you with the same opportunity to demonstrate their skills and aptitudes. As such your answers should relate directly to:

- your understanding of the passage you have read and
- the way in which the author has presented it to you, the reader.

Examine each passage to extract the main ideas and avoid making hasty conclusions.

LNAT® *multiple-choice format*

Section A of the National Admissions Test for Law (LNAT®) contains multiple-choice questions. This section of the test is divided into 12 argumentative passages of text, followed by between three or four multiple-choice questions, to a total of 42 questions. Each of the multiple-choice questions contains five options and only one of these options is correct.

Below is an example of an LNAT® format question.

Prescriptive language

If we were to ask of a person 'What are his moral principles?' the way in which we could be most sure of a true answer would be by studying what he did. He might, to be sure, profess in his conversation all sorts of principles, which in his actions he completely disregarded; but it would be when, knowing all the relevant facts of a situation, he was faced with choices or decisions between alternative courses of action, between alternative answers to the question 'What shall I do?', that he would reveal in what principles of conduct he really believed. The reason why actions are in a peculiar way revelatory of moral principles is that the function of moral principles is to guide conduct. The language of morals is one sort of prescriptive language. And this is what makes ethics worth studying: for the question 'What shall I do?' is one that we cannot for long evade; the problems of conduct, though sometimes less diverting than crossword puzzles, have to be solved in a way that crossword puzzles do not. We cannot wait to see the solution in the next issue, because on the solution of the problems depends what happens in the next issue. Thus, in a world in which the problems of conduct become every day more complex and tormenting, there is a great need for an understanding of the language in which these problems are posed and answered. For confusion about our moral language leads, not merely to theoretical muddles, but to needless practical perplexities.

An old fashioned, but still useful, way of studying anything is *per genus et differentiam*; if moral language belongs to the genus 'prescriptive language', we shall most easily understand its nature if we compare and contrast first of all prescriptive language with other sorts of language, and then moral language with other sorts of prescriptive language.

Source: *The Language of Morals* (R M Hare, Oxford University Press, 1952). By permission of Oxford University Press.

Sample question 1

Which of the following **cannot be inferred** from the passage:

(a) Decision-making reveals what principles of conduct a person really believes

(b) Conduct is guided by moral principles

(c) Theoretical muddles are caused by confusion about our moral language

(d) *Per genus et differentiam* is only one of the number of ways which could be used to study moral language

(e) In relation to morality, actions speak louder than words

Sample question 1: answer and rationale

This question is asking you to look for the negative or a statement that would be false on the basis of the content of the passage. This will be a statement that **cannot be inferred** from statements made in the passage and which does not follow logically from statements made in the passage. The question requires an understanding of inference. An inference is a conclusion drawn from the evidence provided and any statement that meets the criteria would, in this case, be incorrect as the question is asking for a statement that **cannot be inferred**. This type of question needs careful consideration as it amounts, in many cases, to a 'double negative'. The highlighted statement and rationale is correct.

(a) Decision-making reveals what principles of conduct a person really believes

This statement is an incorrect answer as it can be inferred in the passage from the section which states: '...faced with choices or decisions between alternative courses of action, between alternative answers to the question "What shall I do?", that he would reveal in what principles of conduct he really believed'.

(b) Conduct is guided by moral principles

This statement is an incorrect answer as it is directly stated in the passage that: '...the function of moral principles is to guide conduct'.

(c) Theoretical muddles are caused by confusion about our moral language

This statement is an incorrect answer as it is directly stated in the passage that: 'For confusion about our moral language leads, not merely to theoretical muddles, but to needless practical perplexities'.

(d) *Per genus et differentiam* **is only one of the number of ways which could be used to study moral language**

This statement is the correct answer as it cannot be inferred from the information in the passage. The second paragraph of the passage states, 'An old fashioned, but still useful, way of studying anything is *per genus et differentiam;…*' This way of studying applies to anything and not just moral language. There is nothing in the passage that provides any information on any other method or methods for the study of moral language. There may be one method, two, several or even hundreds, but no such information is provided. Therefore, it cannot be inferred there are 'a number of ways' to study moral language.

(e) In relation to morality, actions speak louder than words

This statement is an incorrect answer as it can be inferred in the passage from the phrase: 'He might, to be sure, profess in his conversation all sorts of principles, which in his actions he completely disregarded;…'

Sample question 2

Which of the following is an **unstated assumption** in the passage:

(a) Behaviour is the key to understanding a person's moral principles

(b) Solving a crossword puzzle is not like studying the problems of a person's conduct

(c) Understanding the language used to discuss them provides a better understanding of ethical issues

(d) Moral language is only one type of prescriptive language

(e) Ethics is worth studying because of the language of morals

Sample question 2: answer and rationale

This question is asking you to look for something that is not directly stated in the passage but can be assumed from its content. In making **assumptions** we can take for granted or presuppose something exists even though it is not stated. An **assumption** is something that can be logically inferred from the contents of the passage. However, remember that it must be an **assumption** from the contents of the passage and NOT from your own personal knowledge of a particular subject! The highlighted statement and rationale is correct.

(a) Behaviour is the key to understanding a person's moral principles

This statement is an incorrect answer as it is directly stated in the passage that: 'The reason why actions are in a peculiar way revelatory of moral principles is that the functions of moral principles is to guide conduct.'

(b) Solving a crossword puzzle is not like studying the problems of a person's conduct

This statement is an incorrect answer as it is directly stated in the passage that: '…the problems of conduct, though sometimes less diverting than crossword puzzles, have to be solved in a way that crossword puzzles do not'.

(c) Understanding the language used to discuss them provides a better understanding of ethical issues

This statement is the correct answer as it is an unstated assumption within the passage. Mid-way through the passage it states, 'The language of morals is one sort of prescriptive language. And that is what makes ethics worth studying', but the final paragraph of the passage really provides the answer '…if moral language belongs to the genus "prescriptive language", we shall most easily understand its nature if we compare and contrast first of all prescriptive language with other sorts of language, and then moral language with other sorts of prescriptive language'. From this it can be assumed that 'understanding the language to discuss them provides a better understanding of ethical issues'.

(d) Moral language is only one type of prescriptive language

This statement is an incorrect answer as it is directly stated in the passage that: '…if we compare and contrast…moral language with other sorts of prescriptive language'.

(e) Ethics is worth studying because of the language of morals

This statement is an incorrect answer as it is directly stated in the passage that: 'The language of morals is one sort of prescriptive language. And this is what makes ethics worth studying.'

Sample question 3

Which of the following is the **main** idea in the passage:

(a) Someone's moral principles can be determined by their behaviour

(b) Having a better understanding of the language we use to discuss moral principles

(c) Ethics is an area worth studying

(d) The complexities of the problems of conduct can be resolved by studying moral language

(e) Moral language belongs to the family of prescriptive language

Sample question 3: answer and rationale

This question requires that you can identify the **main** idea in the article. It does not suggest that other ideas will not be present. Again this is an evaluation as to whether the options provided are the **main** idea or not, in other words are they true or false in relation to the question. In order to address this question it will be necessary to read the passage thoroughly in order to follow the ideas and the structure of the argument to reach a conclusion as to which option is the fundamental idea. The passage may contain several points that are pertinent to the overall argument as they help to build up the body of evidence. Therefore, it is important to examine the structure of the argument as this may indicate where the **main** idea is positioned. The highlighted statement and rationale is correct.

(a) Someone's moral principles can be determined by their behaviour

This statement is an incorrect answer as although it is directly stated in the passage that: 'The reason why actions are in a peculiar way revelatory of moral principles is that the function of moral principles is to guide conduct', this is used to inform the reader of a particular area of ethics which is worthy of study. It is not the main idea of the passage but a precursor to it.

(b) Having a better understanding of the language we use to discuss moral principles

This statement is correct because it is the main idea in the passage. This is clearly the most important area and can be found in both the end of the first paragraph and the last paragraph. Towards the end of the first paragraph the passage states, 'Thus, in a world in which the problems of conduct become every day more complex and tormenting, there is a great need for an understanding of the language in which these problems are posed and answered'. In the final paragraph the passage states, '...if moral language belongs to the genus "prescriptive language", we shall most easily understand its nature if we compare and contrast...'.

(c) Ethics is an area worth studying

This statement is an incorrect answer as although it is directly stated in the passage that: 'The language of morals is one sort of prescriptive language. And this is what makes ethics worth studying', it is just a part, albeit an important part, of the overall passage leading up to the main idea of the way in which moral language can be studied.

(d) The complexities of the problems of conduct can be resolved by studying moral language

This statement is an incorrect answer as although the passage refers to '...the problems of conduct become every day more complex...', it does not directly or indirectly state or infer or assume anywhere that such complexities can be resolved by studying moral language. Because the statement is 'false' in relation to the passage it cannot be the main idea.

(e) Moral language belongs to the family of prescriptive language

This statement is an incorrect answer as although it is stated in the passage that: '… if moral language belongs to the genus "prescriptive language"…', this only provides part of the context in which the study of moral language can be undertaken.

7. Developing critical reasoning test skills

You may have found the sample questions a little daunting. One reason for that might be that you will have fallen into the trap of 'speed reading' or skimming the quoted passage simply because it will, by this stage in your education, have become almost second nature. There will still be occasions in your further studies – even in law – where skim reading is appropriate. However, for the purposes of the LNAT® and the exercises that follow in this book, the words have been chosen deliberately and require careful consideration.

Before attempting the practice questions based on the approach taken in the LNAT® you should find it beneficial to work through the questions in this section. The commencing passages and questions presented below are formatted along similar lines to commercially produced tests of verbal critical reasoning, which generally use standardised response options of true, false or cannot determine. The final passage and questions will replicate the style and format of the LNAT®. The answers and the rationales for the correct answers follow each question. In addition, because it is as helpful to know why you may have answered some questions incorrectly the LNAT® format question is also followed by the reasons why the alternative answers are incorrect. This staged approach should develop your understanding of how critical reasoning tests are structured and should also develop your confidence and ability when answering the questions.

The first passage is a relatively short paragraph followed by just one question. Subsequent passages will increase in size and the number of questions will increase to a maximum of three. The final passage and questions will serve as a 'trial run' prior to attempting the 'LNAT® practice test' section of the book.

Passage and response formats

The passages are extracts taken from various books, magazines, periodicals and newspapers. Each of the passages includes statements and arguments that are intended to convey information, or to persuade the reader of a point of view. Remember to assume that what is stated in the passages is factual and avoid drawing on your knowledge of any of the topics, which may contradict that of the author. Drawing on this assumption, read the passage carefully and decide whether the statement or statements are true or false or cannot determine.

The definitions to be applied to each statement are:

- *True*: This means that the statement is actually made in the passage, that it is implied, or follows logically from the information in the passage.

- *False*: This means that the statement directly contradicts a statement made in, implied by, or that follows logically from the passage.

- *Cannot determine*: This means that there is insufficient information in the passage to arrive at a firm conclusion as to whether the statement is true or false.

Note that the LNAT® will only be concerned with the identity of **true** and **false** statements i.e. for every passage one of the five options will be true and the other four will be false. In the examples below a 'cannot determine' feature is used which is a typical feature of many commercially available verbal reasoning tests. This will be useful in preparing you for these types of test. LNAT® format passages and questions are contained in Section 8 of Part II, which immediately follows this section, where the 'cannot determine' response becomes redundant.

Passage 1: student places

Oxford University is planning to cut hundreds of places for British undergraduates and increase those for foreign students as it aims to stem chronic losses that threaten its world-class status.

The university admitted that it was in effect being bailed out by profits from the Oxford University Press, which covered an annual £20 million deficit on teaching and research in 2003. A strategy paper concluded: 'The available evidence suggests that if radical measures are not taken, Oxford's standing will decline.'

Oxford's plans underline the dilemma facing Britain's top universities. Members of the Russell Group of 19 research-intensive universities have given warning repeatedly that the increase in tuition fees to £3,000 a year from next year is insufficient to meet global competition.

Source: 'Funding crisis forces Oxford to cut British student places' (Tony Haplin, *Times*, 25 January 2005). © The *Times*.

Passage 1: question 1
Oxford University receives more income from foreign students than from British undergraduates.

(a) True   (b) False   (c) Cannot Determine

Answer: True.

Although the statement is not actually made in the passage it does follow logically from those statements that *are* made in the passage. The fact that Oxford University is planning to cut places for British undergraduates and increase those for foreign students as it aims to stem chronic losses clearly implies that more money is received from foreign students. The passage then justifies the need for the student profile changes by detailing financial deficits on teaching and research, which have to be addressed, and also implies that the income is greater from foreign students.

Passage 2: judicial review

Judicial review is a method of challenging decisions made by administrative bodies and office holders such as the police service. Cases can range from policy decisions made by the organisation – such as the decision not to prosecute someone – to decisions made by individual supervisors (e.g. the cautioning of a juvenile). The circumstances under which a matter can go before the High Court for judicial review are quite limited. Generally, applications for judicial review can only proceed if there is no other method by which to appeal the decision. An application for judicial review must be made as soon as reasonably practicable and generally within three months of the decision. In reviewing the decision the High Court can look at whether the administrative body or individual was acting within the law when making that decision; it will also consider whether the decision was a reasonable one and whether the common law rules of natural justice were applied.

Whether a decision was made within the law will be determined by a number of features surrounding the decision-making process. These would include:

- Whether the organisation or individual actually had the authority or power to make the decision.
- What procedure was followed and whether that procedure observed the requirements of 'natural justice'.
- Whether the decision-maker exercised his/her own discretion or whether he/she delegated or fettered that discretion in a way which was not permitted in law.

Source: *Blackstone's Police Manual. Volume 2. Evidence and Procedure* (Oxford University Press, 2005). © Glenn Hutton and David Johnston, 2005. By permission of Oxford University Press.

Passage 2: question 1

When all other methods by which to appeal a decision have been made the matter can go before the High Court for judicial review.

(a) True   (b) False   (c)   Cannot Determine

Answer: False.

The statement cannot be implied from statements made in the passage and does not follow logically from statements made in the passage. The passage does state that applications for judicial review generally only proceed if other methods by which to appeal a decision are not possible. It does not state that judicial review will proceed if all other methods have been applied. In addition, the passage clearly states criteria that have to be met in order to determine whether a decision was made within the law and whether the common law rules of justice were applied.

Passage 2: question 2

All applications for judicial review must be made within three months of the decision.

(a) True   (b) False   (c) Cannot Determine

Answer: Cannot Determine.

There is insufficient information in the passage to arrive at a firm conclusion as to whether the statement is true or false. The passage states that: 'An application for judicial review must be made as soon as reasonably practicable and generally within three months of the decision.' It is possible that, although made outside of three months, an application may be deemed to have been made as soon as was 'reasonably practicable'. However, on the other hand the three months deadline may be applied to all applications. Therefore, this statement cannot be classified as true or false from the passage without further information regarding the actual practice of judicial review.

Passage 3: space flight

Scientists weigh up merits of manned missions

British scientists will meet this week to thrash out an answer to a question that has caused argument for decades: is it worth sending humans into space?

The Royal Astronomical Society (RAS) has called upon three wise men of science – Professor Frank Close, an Oxford University physicist, Professor Ken Pounds, an astrophysicist from the University of Leicester and Dr John Dudeney, deputy director of the British Antarctic Survey in Cambridge – to weigh up the scientific arguments for and against human space flight and report back when they have reached a conclusion.

The question will become increasingly important in the next year or so. President Bush has already asked NASA to develop a programme to build a manned moon base as a precursor to sending astronauts to Mars. Meanwhile, the European Space Agency's ambitious Aurora project has scheduled a series of robotic missions to Mars with the intention of landing an astronaut on the planet by 2033.

Last year, the science minister, David Sainsbury, pledged £5 million to join the Aurora programme, but said Britain would not support a manned mission.

The three scientists will have the first of a series of meetings on Friday at the RAS offices in London. 'The broad question we'll be looking at is will having people in space materially advance our knowledge in ways that would otherwise be impossible or extremely unlikely,' said Prof Close.

Critics of crewed space missions point to expensive projects such as the $100bn (£53bn) International Space Station and the loss of two space shuttles and their crews in accidents in 1986 and 2003 as evidence that the benefits to science do not justify the cost or risk of putting humans in space. Others argue that humans can do far more useful science in space than robotic probes.

Source: 'Humans or robots? UK ponders future of space flight' (Ian Sample, *Guardian*, 24 January 2005). © *The Guardian*.

Passage 3: question 1

The decision as to whether humans will be sent into space again rests with three British scientists.

(a) True   (b) False   (c) Cannot Determine

Answer: False.

The statement cannot be implied from statements made in the passage and does not follow logically from statements made in the passage. The three British scientists mentioned in the passage have been appointed by The Royal Astronomical Society (RAS) to weigh up the pros and cons of human space flight and to report back. However, the passage neither states nor implies that humans will not be sent into space as a result of their findings. The passage does state that manned space flight programmes planned by NASA and the European Space Agency are already in progress. The fact that Britain will not support a manned Aurora mission does not imply that it will not happen.

Passage 3: question 2

Humans are more competent at scientific research in space than robots.

(a) True   (b) False   (c) Cannot Determine

Answer: Cannot Determine.

There is insufficient information in the passage to arrive at a firm conclusion as to whether the statement is true or false. The passage does not state or imply that humans are better at scientific research in space than robots. The main point of the passage is to weigh up the merits of manned space missions. Part of the assessment of this will be to determine what advances can be made in terms of scientific knowledge by using humans as opposed to robotic probes. In other words, the value of humans over robots or vice versa has yet to be determined.

Passage 3: question 3

Scientific advancement is impossible or extremely unlikely without cost or loss of life.

(a) True   (b) False   (c) Cannot Determine

Answer: False.

The statement cannot be implied from statements made in the passage and does not follow logically from statements made in the passage. The passage does criticise the high costs in terms of finance and loss of lives attributed to space projects but this does not imply that all scientific advancement results in such costs.

Passage 4: geology and classification

A system of classification of plants and animals (both fossil and living) that can be universally applied is of central importance to natural science. Even if we draw back from the view that natural science is nothing more than the relentless working through of the task of classification, we can agree that science cannot proceed beyond local or regional curiosity without general systems. In the early nineteenth century, as the speed of new discoveries threatened to overtake the adoption of universal concepts, the problem of classification became acute. Scientists, being pragmatic, realised that a solution was urgently required. One system of classification began to be favoured above others, and rapidly became the most widely adopted. Martin Simpson, Curator at Whitby Museum for most of the second half of the nineteenth century, and one of the pioneers of fossil taxonomy, explains the difficulty:

'In drawing up a Descriptive Catalogue of the Fossils of the Yorkshire Lias, I without hesitation adopt the views of the late Baron Cuvier, which I consider to be by far the most comprehensive, the simplest, and the most instructive, of any which have yet been promulgated on the classification of animals. Whilst the system of Cuvier, founded upon the strictest, and most perfect anatomical investigations, embraces and unites, both the systems of Aristotle and Linnaeus, his principles of nomenclature, seem to me the best calculated to rescue natural history, from that confusion into which it has unhappily fallen. By adopting the comprehensive generic groups of Linnaeus, as genera, thousands of names which now becloud and perplex natural history, might be rendered either very subordinate, or entirely swept away. And by adopting such genera as those of Lamarck, as sub-genera, or divisions of genera, the species can be the more easily described and understood. Also by this method naturalists having different views of nomenclature, might still understand each other. For whilst the followers of Cuvier and Linnaeus would adopt the names of the more comprehensive groups, as the names of their genera, others might prefer the names of smaller groups, for generic names, as those of Lamarck; yet both parties would understand each other; the sub-genus being merely a division of the genus. If, however, naturalists will go on multiplying generic names of but little importance, in the great system of nature, and often worse than synonymous, the prediction of Cuvier will be verified: – That the advantages of the binomial system so happily imagined by Linnaeus will be lost; and geologists, and men of general learning, will in a great measure be excluded from pursuing the details of Natural History; the number of genera being already far beyond any ordinary man's comprehension.'

Source: *The Floating Egg* (Roger Osborne, Jonathan Cape, 1998). Reprinted by permission of The Random House Group Ltd.

Passage 4: question 1

All natural history scientists have adopted Baron Cuvier's principles of nomenclature.

(a) True   (b) False   (c) Cannot Determine

Answer: False.

The statement cannot be implied from statements made in the passage and does not follow logically from statements made in the passage. It is stated in the first paragraph that: 'One system of classification began to be favoured above others, and rapidly became the most widely adopted.' Classification is a synonym of nomenclature and by reading further in the passage it is clear this statement refers to the system of Cuvier. However, the passage does not state or imply that all Natural History scientists have adopted Cuvier's principles of nomenclature, although it does imply that a large number have.

Passage 4: question 2

Martin Simpson, Curator at Whitby Museum for most of the second half of the nineteenth century, adopted a system of fossil taxonomy based on genera and sub-genera.

(a) True   (b) False   (c) Cannot Determine

Answer: True.

Although the statement is not expressly made in the passage, it nevertheless follows logically from statements made in the passage. Taxonomy is synonymous with classification and the main point of this passage is to support the views of Cuvier, which were adopted by Martin Simpson when classifying fossils. The passage describes Cuvier's binominal system as being based on the adoption of Aristotle's and Linnaeus's generic groups as genera and the adoption of Lamarck's genera as sub-genera.

Passage 4: question 3

A species is of a higher rank in the taxonomy of plants and animals (both fossil and living) than a genus and sub-genus.

(a) True (b) False (c) Cannot Determine

Answer: False.

The statement cannot be implied from statements made in the passage and does not follow logically from statements made in the passage. The passage, towards the end, clearly states that 'the sub-genus being merely a division of the genus'. It is also explicit in the passage that a species can be more easily described and understood when we know the genera and sub-genera (which are merely plurals of genus and sub-genus). Therefore, it is clear from the passage that species are ranked lower in the taxonomy of plants and animals.

Passage 5: analogical problem-solving and learning

The book began with a review of research on human problem-solving on a number of very simple, puzzle-like transformation problems such as the Towers of Hanoi. The research on transfer of learning discussed in Part I revealed that people may experience considerable difficulty in transferring what they know about solving a problem of a particular type when they are confronted with a new problem of the same type. The research showed that subjects sometimes had to be told the relationship between two problems before they could apply previously acquired knowledge in solving a new problem, and even then previous experience was no help if the new problem was more complex than the earlier one.

Another way of conceptualising the problem of transfer between problems is to ask whether people can see the analogies between similar problems and can exploit these to solve novel problems.

In Part II we found conflicting evidence about people's ability to exploit analogies between similar problems. On the one hand, Gick and Holyoak's research on the radiation problem indicates that people are unlikely to use a prior analogy (the fortress problem) unless they are given a hint to do so. Nevertheless, they are quite successful at using analogies once the idea has been suggested to them. On the other hand, the results of experiments conducted by Reed, Dempster and Ettinger on students' ability to use worked-out solutions of algebra problems suggest that people may experience considerable difficulty in applying analogies in more realistic, classroom situations. Taken together, the findings indicate that people are rather poor at transferring knowledge from one situation to another without considerable guidance. This conclusion is supported by the results of research reported in Part II in which it was shown that experimental subjects were unlikely to construct and abstract schema for similar problems unless they were presented with at least a couple of closely related problems, and provided with information on the principle that unites them.

All this has considerable implications for learning, since most teaching is based on the notion that students can learn to extract general principles from problem-solving experiences which they can apply to solve other similar problems.

So, what can we learn from problem-solving research about how to design teaching materials? Textbooks on subjects such as mathematics, physics or computer programming usually contain a number of main sections in which principles are defined and discussed. Principles are sometimes illustrated with a worked-out example. Students are then presented with a number of practice problems which are designed to provide the student with the know-how to apply the principles to all problems of that type.

Research into analogical problem solving, though, suggests that the relationship between the original worked-out example and the exercise problems should not be left to students to puzzle out for themselves, but should be made explicit. Although this might seem just plain common sense, the fact is that many textbook writers do not employ such principles. For example, I know of one standard textbook on computer programming in which exercise problems bear only the most tenuous relationship with the worked-out examples used for teaching purposes in earlier parts of the text. When considering an example situation closer at hand, students often find it difficult to fit worked examples of statistical tests to the data analysis they are currently handling, even when the worked examples are extremely detailed.

Source *Problem Solving: Current Issues* (second edition, Hank Kahney, Open University Press, 1993). © The Open University. By kind permission of the Open University Press/McGraw-Hill Publishing Company.

Passage 5: question 1

People are likely to solve a problem just as well as each other if they are given the analogy between that problem and a similar problem.

(a) True   (b) False   (c) Cannot Determine

Answer: Cannot Determine.

There is insufficient information in the passage to arrive at a firm conclusion as to whether the statement is true or false. The quoted research showed that subjects sometimes had to be told the relationship between two problems before they could apply previously acquired knowledge in solving a new problem, and even then previous experience was of no help if the new problem was more complex than the earlier one. It does not discuss the difference in performance of those who are given the analogy to a similar level problem.

Passage 5: question 2

Problem-solving skills are generally transferable when the schema for a problem is almost identical to previously experienced problems.

(a) True   (b) False   (c) Cannot Determine

Answer: False.

The statement cannot be implied from statements made in the passage and does not follow logically from statements made in the passage. It is stated (at the end of the third paragraph) 'that experimental subjects were unlikely to construct and abstract schema for similar problems unless they were presented with at least a couple of closely related problems'. On the basis of this it could be suggested that the statement is true; however, the statement goes on to add that they also need to be 'provided with information on the principle that unites them'. This would suggest that they are generally unable to transfer problem-solving skills without the links being made explicit.

Passage 5: question 3

If analogies are explicitly stated for any type of problem in the form of worked-out examples then all students should be able to solve any type of problem.

(a) True   (b) False   (c) Cannot Determine

Answer: False.

The statement cannot be implied from statements made in the passage and does not follow logically from statements made in the passage. The research in the passage does suggest that the relationship between a worked-out example and the exercise problem should be made explicit in order for students to successfully solve the new problem. However, it also states that students often find it difficult to use the analogies from detailed examples when applying statistical tests to data analysis or other more complex problems. Therefore, there may be some problems that some students would still not solve.

8. LNAT® response formats

The questions relating to the passage below have been designed to replicate the style used in the LNAT®. Each set of statements will be preceded by a question, which will define the criteria for evaluating the statements. For example, you may be asked to determine: whether a statement is inferred or not inferred in the passage; which statement is the main idea of the passage or part of the passage; what the writer means by a particular phrase in the passage; which statement is a stated or unstated assertion or assumption in the passage etc. Basically, you are still being asked to evaluate the truth or falsity of the statements in light of the given criteria in each question.

Passage 6: house arrest

Senior lawyers last night criticised the home secretary's plan for a new control order to be imposed on British and foreign terrorist suspects and called on him to think again.

Concerns focused on the plan to allow house arrest in serious cases, the low threshold – reasonable grounds to suspect involvement in terrorism – and the fact that there would be no time limit.

The new orders would be imposed by the home secretary, but could be challenged in front of a judge. Conditions under such an order could include surrendering a passport, curfew, electronic tagging, reporting regularly to police, limits on use of the telephone and the internet and, in the most serious cases, house arrest.

Guy Mansfield QC, chairman of the bar, said: 'I remain concerned that suspicion is apparently to be sufficient to detain individuals. I would ask parliament to consider this with great care. The proposed control orders should be evaluated on their merits and case by case. Disproportionate measures risk radicalising the community from which a detainee comes. That may make this country less rather than more safe.'

Ian Macdonald QC, who resigned as a special advocate – a barrister appointed by the government to represent detainees before the Special Immigration Appeal Tribunal – said: 'House arrest is detention by another name. It would require a derogation. That raises the question of how long is an emergency. Why is it that no other country which faces the same threat has done the same sort of thing?'

He criticised the 'reasonable grounds to suspect' threshold and said those placed under an order – like the detainees at present – would have no right to know evidence against them and therefore no means of challenging it.

'Take the Tipton Three who were supposed to have met Bin Laden in a camp on such-and-such a date. It turned out that on that date they were all in Tipton and one of them was working on the checkout in Currys,' he said. 'Under this procedure they wouldn't get the information and the guy wouldn't know that it's ever been suggested he's been to some camp. Yet it would be there and he wouldn't be able to contest it.'

It is widely believed Charles Clarke will face another lengthy court battle if he imposes the house arrest orders.

The legislation will allow Mr Clarke to place foreign and British nationals reasonably suspected of terrorism under control orders. Lawyers said the men sent back from Guantanamo Bay could have such orders placed on them.

Article 5 of the European Human Rights Convention lays down only limited circumstances under which a person may be deprived of liberty. When a member of the Italian mafia was required to live on a tiny island for 18 months while awaiting trial, the European Court of Human Rights in Strasbourg held that he had been denied his human rights.

The measures aim to meet objections that part 4 of the Anti-Terrorism, Crime and Security Act 2001, which allows indefinite detention for foreign terror suspects, breaches human rights laws. The law lords threw Britain's anti-terror policy into disarray when they said indefinite detention without trial for foreign suspects alone was disproportionate and discriminatory.

Source: 'New house arrest plan criticised' (Clare Dyer, *Guardian*, 27 January 2005). © *The Guardian.*

Passage 6: question 1

Which of these **cannot be inferred** from the passage?

(a) House arrest would require the curtailment of an application of the existing law

(b) The restriction of freedom is limited

(c) British nationals suspected of terrorism have a right to know the evidence held against them

(d) The internet is a communication method often used by terrorists

(e) An act of terrorism would not have to be committed for a person to be placed under house arrest

Passage 6: question 1 – answer and rationale

This question is asking you to look for the negative or a statement that would be false on the basis of the content of the passage. This will be a statement that **cannot be inferred** from statements made in the passage and which does not follow logically from statements made in the passage. The question requires an understanding of inference. An inference is a conclusion drawn from the evidence provided and any statement that meets the criteria would, in this case, be incorrect as the question is asking for a statement that **cannot be inferred**. This type of question needs careful consideration as it amounts, in many cases, to a 'double negative'. The highlighted statement and rationale is correct.

(a) House arrest would require the curtailment of an application of the law

This statement is an incorrect answer as it is directly stated in the passage that: 'House arrest is detention by another name. It would require a derogation'. In other words it would necessitate a change to existing law.

(b) The restriction of freedom is limited

This statement is an incorrect answer as it is directly stated in the passage that: 'the European Human Rights Convention lays down only limited circumstances under which a person may be deprived of liberty'. Therefore, the restriction of freedom is limited by human rights legislation.

(c) British nationals suspected of terrorism have a right to know the evidence held against them

This statement is an incorrect answer as it can be inferred from information in the passage. Current British law gives British nationals suspected of terrorism the right to know the evidence held against them. The passage relates to the case of the Tipton Three who were able to contest information held against them which they would not be allowed access to under the proposed new controls. The passage also implies that they are British nationals because they would not have been allowed access to this information under the Anti-Terrorism, Crime and Security Act 2001 if they were foreign terror suspects, which is a point made at the end of the passage.

(d) The internet is a communication method often used by terrorists

This statement is the correct answer as it cannot be inferred from the information in the passage. It is suggested in the passage that the conditions attached to the proposed new control order may include the limitation of internet access. However, it cannot be directly inferred from this that terrorists often use the internet as a means of communication. It could be made as an assertion generally – and you may know this from your own experience – but there is no evidence in the passage to support this claim.

(e) An act of terrorism would not have to be committed for a person to be placed under house arrest

This is an incorrect answer as it does not state in the passage that an act of terrorism has to be committed but that there are 'reasonable grounds to suspect involvement in terrorism', and 'that suspicion is apparently to be sufficient to detain individuals'. It is explicit that an act of terrorism would not have to be committed.

Passage 6: question 2

Which of the following is the **main** idea in the article?

(a) Suspicion of terrorism is sufficient to detain British and foreign suspects

(b) The proposed new control order is a controversial legal issue

(c) A disproportionate new control order may make this country more vulnerable

(d) Britain's anti-terror policy has been thrown into disarray

(e) British as well as foreign terrorist suspects will be affected by the proposed new control order

Passage 6: question 2 – answer and rationale

This question requires that you can identify the **main** idea in the article. It does not suggest that other ideas will not be present. Again this is an evaluation as to whether the options provided are the **main** idea or not, in other words are they true or false in relation to the question. In order to address this question it will be necessary to read the passage thoroughly in order to follow the ideas and the structure of the argument to reach a conclusion as to which option is the fundamental idea. The passage may contain several points that are pertinent to the overall argument as they help to build up the body of evidence. Therefore, it is important to examine the structure of the argument as this may indicate where the **main** idea is positioned. The highlighted statement and rationale is correct.

(a) Suspicion of terrorism is sufficient to detain British and foreign suspects

This answer is incorrect as it is not the main idea in the passage. The writer mentions the expressed concerns that the suspicion of terrorism may be sufficient to detain individuals but this is only cited as part of the overall argument, albeit a significant part.

(b) The proposed new control order is a controversial legal issue

This answer is correct, as it is the main idea in the passage. The passage commences with concerns expressed by senior lawyers, regarding the new control order, which are developed throughout the passage. The writer also comments on the lengthy court battles that may ensue if Charles Clarke imposes house arrest orders. The controversy surrounding the legality of the proposed control order is further supported by the law lords' comments at the end of the passage.

(c) A disproportionate new control order may make this country more vulnerable

This answer is incorrect as it is not the main idea in the passage. This point of view is expressed in the passage by Ian Macdonald QC as being one of the factors that may make the proposed control order controversial; it is used as a possible outcome of the imposition of disproportionate measures and it is not supported throughout the passage as a key issue.

(d) Britain's anti-terror policy has been thrown into disarray

This answer is incorrect as it is not the main idea in the passage. This statement made at the end of the passage is used as an important example as to why the proposed new control order is controversial. It relates to the current practice, under the Anti-Terrorism, Crime and Security Act 2001, which allows the indefinite detention of foreign terror suspects and claims that this is disproportionate and discriminatory.

(e) British as well as foreign terrorist suspects will be affected by the proposed new control order

This answer is incorrect as it is not the main idea in the passage. Whilst this statement is true it is not the central idea of the passage. The possible impact the proposed new control order will have on British nationals is discussed in the passage and it is clearly of great concern. However, the concerns expressed in the passage have far wider implications for both current and proposed changes to legislation.

Passage 6: question 3

Which of the following is **implied** but not directly stated by the writer:

(a) Detainees come from radical communities

(b) Freedom is a human right

(c) Long confinements of terror suspects without trial may breach human rights

(d) Electronic tagging is preferable to house arrest

(e) A new control order should not contravene existing laws

Passage 6: question 3 – answer and rationale

This question is asking you to identify which statement is **implied** but not directly stated in the passage but does follow logically from statements made in the passage. Again you are looking for which of the options is true or false (correct or incorrect) given the question. There are two types of statements that would be incorrect. The first type of potential answer would be one where the proposition is directly stated as the question asks you to identify issues which are not directly stated. It follows that anything that is explicit (actually stated) must be incorrect in the light of the instruction you have been given in this particular question.

It is important to remember that explicit or stated does not necessarily mean that the statement will appear verbatim (word for word). What it does mean is that the option should be a clear statement, which means precisely the same as something which is 'stated in the passage'.

The second type of answer that would be incorrect would be a statement that does not form part of the argument for whatever reason. The highlighted statement and rationale is correct.

(a) Detainees come from radical communities

This answer is incorrect as it is not implied in the passage. This statement is a mis-reading and a mis-interpretation of the text. It is stated that 'disproportionate measures risk radicalising the community from which a detainee comes' – this does not imply that detainees come from radical communities.

(b) Freedom is a human right

This answer is incorrect as it is not implied in the passage. This statement is irrelevant as the article is arguing about the impact the controversial proposed control order would have on terror suspects – it is not arguing about the right to freedom for all.

(c) Long confinements of terror suspects without trial may breach human rights

This answer is incorrect as it is not implied in the passage. In fact, this option is actually stated in the last paragraph.

(d) Electronic tagging is preferable to house arrest

This answer is incorrect as it is not implied in the passage. This statement is irrelevant as the article states that two of the conditions of the proposed new control order are electronic tagging and in the most serious cases, house arrest – it does not argue the case for which is preferable.

(e) A new control order should not contravene existing laws

This answer is correct as it can be implied from the passage. Although not explicitly stated in the article it is clearly part of the argument put forward in the article that new laws are subject to existing laws. In addition, this answer can be arrived at through a process of elimination as all the other options are incorrect.

Part III
LNAT® Practice Test and Answers

9. LNAT® practice test

This chapter relates to **Section A** of the LNAT®. It is an on-screen test which consists of 12 separate passages of text with each passage followed by between three and four multiple-choice questions. There is a total of 42 multiple-choice questions and the time allowed for the test is 95 minutes. The screen you will be presented with is split; the relevant passage of text appears in the left-hand pane and the associated questions in the right-hand pane. A scroll facility is provided where the text is longer than the screen. When you have decided which is the correct answer you click a button on the screen next to that answer. You will only be able to choose one answer at a time and you may change your answer to any of the questions during the duration of this part of the test. The system also allows you to flag any questions which you have either failed or found difficult to answer so that you can return to them later. The time remaining for the test is displayed in the top right-hand corner of the screen.

The practice questions in this chapter replicate those used in the LNAT® but it is a decision for you as to whether you time constrain their completion to the 95 minutes. It might be more appropriate to use the practice test in developing your knowledge and skills. The two practice tests provided on the LNAT® website might be better used to judge time management and also provide the experience of sitting the test on-screen.

Before completing this section it might be useful to refresh your memory as to the two suggested strategies often used in answering these types of questions. The strategies can be found on page 14. Maybe try using both strategies for different questions and see which one suits you best.

The test is not a test of knowledge but of fundamental intellectual skills. Do not use your knowledge of a particular issue when answering any of the questions.

Remember each question has a possible choice of five answers and only ONE answer is correct.

After the practice questions, Section 10 of Part III provides an answer matrix and then examines the rationale for both the correct and incorrect answers.

Passage 1: Oxbridge prejudice?

It is no secret that there aren't huge numbers of students from working-class backgrounds studying at the most prestigious universities. Eight of the 10 universities with the lowest proportions of working-class students were in the prestigious Russell Group of research-intensive universities.

With just 11.5% of its intake coming from working-class families, Oxford is bottom in this particular table and Cambridge is next with 12.6%. In addition to this suggested under-representation of working-class students, Oxford and Cambridge are also fending off allegations of racial exclusion after it was revealed that 21 of their colleges made no offers to black students last year.

A request made under the Freedom of Information (FoI) Act by a fellow Labour MP has painted a bleak portrait of racial and social exclusion at Oxbridge institutions. Official data shows that more than 20 Oxbridge colleges made no offers to black candidates for undergraduate courses last year and one Oxford college has not admitted a single black student in five years, and just three in the past decade.

Figures revealed in requests made under the FoI Act also show that Oxford's social profile is 89% upper- and middle-class, while 87.6% of the Cambridge student body is drawn from the top three socioeconomic groups. The average for British universities is 64.5%, according to the admissions body UCAS. The FoI data also shows that of more than 1,500 academic and lab staff at Cambridge, none are black. Thirty-four are of British Asian origin.

Eleven Oxford colleges and 10 Cambridge colleges made no offers to black students for the academic year beginning last autumn. A total of 77 students of Indian descent were accepted, out of 466 applications. Six black Caribbean undergraduates were accepted at Cambridge the same year. But the FoI data shows white students were more likely to be successful than black applicants at every Cambridge college except St Catharine's, where black candidates have had a 38% success rate, compared with 30% for white students.

The starkest divide in Cambridge was at Newnham, an all-women's college, where black applicants had a 13% success rate compared with 67% for white students. The data for Oxford tells a similar story: at Jesus College white candidates were three and a half times more successful than black candidates over an 11-year period. Oxford says the figures are too low for the variation between colleges to be statistically significant.

The most selective universities argue that poor attainment at school level narrows the pool from which candidates can be drawn and that black candidates are more likely to apply to elite universities. An Oxford spokesman informed me that black students apply disproportionately for the most oversubscribed subjects, contributing to a lower than average success rate for the group as a whole. He added that colleges make offers to the best and brightest students regardless of their background, and where variations exist this is due to supply of applications and demand by subject.

Passage 1: Oxbridge prejudice questions

1   This passage is an extract from a speech. To **whom** do you think the speech was addressed?

(a) Oxbridge lecturers

(b) Student applicants

(c) Parents

(d) Politicians

(e) Commission for Racial Equality

2   Which one of the following is an **assertion of fact** rather than **opinion**?

(a) 'An Oxford spokesman informed me'

(b) 'where variations exist this is due to supply of applications and demand by subject'

(c) 'the figures are too low for the variation between colleges to be statistically signifiant'

(d) 'poor attainment at school level narrows the pool'

(e) 'black candidates are more likely to apply to elite universities'

3   Which of the following does the writer **imply** but **not state**?

(a) Black students are less intelligent compared to white students.

(b) That Oxford and Cambridge select on the basis of class as well as attainment

(c) Working-class students are still under-represented in British universities.

(d) White students are over five times more successful than black students at Newnham College, Cambridge

(e) Research-intensive universities are not attractive to working-class students

4   It might be suggested from the passage that the following provide evidence of prejudice at Oxbridge institutions, **except**:

(a) '...21 of their colleges made no offers to black students last year.'

(b) '...there aren't huge numbers of students from working-class backgrounds...'

(c) '...of more than 1,500 academic and lab staff at Cambridge, none are black.'

(d) '...white candidates were three and a half times more successful than black candidates over an 11-year period.'

(e) '...where variations exist this is due to supply of applications and demand by subject.'

Passage 2: *media technologies and children*

Traditionally young people's relationship with digital new media has been characterised as either seeing children as the victims of such technology, encouraged to indulge in violent computer games and helpless to the hypnotic power of the screen, or as canny 'cyber citizens' of the digital generation. Prensky (2001) refers to all such young people as 'digital natives', empowered by technology to discover and even create new worlds of communication and learning.

The 'educational' promise of new media technology is seen by some as beneficial, but the 'entertainment' such technologies can provide is condemned by others as both culturally worthless and even morally damaging (Sigman, 2007).

For many, the idea of children watching television as a positive occupation is unconvincing. However, when considering the positive links between television, language development and the curriculum for the Foundation Stage in England, a study by Marsh et al. (2005) identified that television viewing, in the right circumstances, can help pre-school children to be able to:

● use words, gestures, simple questions or statements;

● listen to nursery rhymes, stories and songs, joining in with repeated refrains;

● enjoy listening to and using spoken language;

● sustain attentive listening;

● respond to extended vocabulary;

● explore the meaning and sounds of new words; use language to recreate experiences;

● use talk to clarify thinking, ideas, feeling and events;

- link sounds to letters;
- begin to be aware of the way stories are structured.

Research by Bazalgette (2003) found that children who watched television understood image sequences as well as a combination of images and sound. This understanding of media could be transferred to the written word.

Other research by Kremer et al. (2002) suggested that there may be 'text level' concepts, for example genre and narrative structure, which are not restricted to print literacy, which can be developed through the engagement with quality screen viewing; these skills being transferable to print literacy.

In relation to writing Parker (1999) looked at the relationship between creative work and moving images and children's writing. The writing produced by children demonstrated that the children who had worked with animations produced written work, which contained more detail, depth and character empathy.

Source: *Education Studies: The impact of new media technologies* (by Elizabeth Hopkins, Learning Matters Ltd, 2009). © Elizabeth Hopins. By kind permission of Learning Matters Ltd.

Passage 2: media technologies and children questions

5 According to the passage what is the **main disadvantage** of media technology?

   (a) Young children are the victims of media technology

   (b) Media technology encourages violence

   (c) Media technology can be damaging to young people

   (d) Media technology is hypnotic

   (e) Media technology is inferior to books

6 Which is the **most significant** point of the quoted research?

   (a) Media technology helps children develop language and writing skills

   (b) Skills developed through the use of media technology are transferable

   (c) Children taught using media technology are more creative in their written work

   (d) The vocabulary of children can be increased by television viewing

   (e) Children respond well to media technology.

7 What is the **main** purpose of this passage?

(a) To promote the use of media technology in schools

(b) To drag education into the twenty-first century

(c) To quote the pros and cons of media technology

(d) To inform teachers of the potential benefits from the use of media technology

(e) To support the financial investment that has been made in technology within schools

Passage 3: stereotyping

Lippman (1922) popularised the phrase 'stereotype' and explained the term by describing it as referring to the 'pictures in our heads' we have of people. Lippman viewed stereotypes as being a means whereby people protect their relative standing in society. Deaux and Lewis (1983) used this understanding of stereotype in relation to western attitudes about men and women. Whereas men are considered to be 'independent and competitive' women are seen as being 'warm and emotional'. Linssen and Hagendoorn (1994) have developed this work in relation to European students' stereotypical images of northern and southern European characteristics. Whereas northern nations have been perceived as being 'efficient' southern Europeans are identified as being 'characterised by emotion'.

Stereotyping in itself is not necessarily negative. It is something that all of us engage in to form our views of the world. Nevertheless, it may also be argued that stereotyping is the cause of many prejudicial attitudes. At the centre of the prejudicial attitude is the process of labelling negative attributes to particular individuals.

You might say that prejudice is something inside the individual, perhaps an inborn personality trait that eventually manifests itself later in life and causes the person to hold discriminating attitudes towards certain groups in society. Alternatively you might think that prejudice arises against other people when we realise that they hold different, contradictory views to our own. In this case prejudice would not be part of personality but would be seen as a consequence of this realisation of difference between yourself and others. You might also think that prejudice and conflict are the inevitable result of our being part of a particular social group. For example, if you consider yourself to be a socialist you would automatically experience prejudicial views towards those who identify themselves as leaning towards the political right wing.

Albert Bandura (1977) popularised the idea that behaviour is imitated or 'modelled' if there exists a strong emotional attachment to the person exhibiting the behaviour. If this is the case, Malim and Birch (1998) suggest it is possible to predict that prejudicial attitudes will be reinforced within social groups who have a strong emotional bond. It can be argued that racism is a form of learned behaviour that is likely to be copied when individuals share close emotional bonds with other peers who put their prejudicial actions into effect.

Source: *Applied Psychology for Social Work: What is a stereotype?* (by Ewan Ingleby, Learning Matters Ltd 2006). © Ewan Ingleby. By kind permission of Learning Matters Ltd.

Passage 3: stereotyping questions

8 Which of the following phrases **best defines** a stereotype?

  (a) An image or conception of others that is shared by all members of a social group

  (b) A set of generalisations about an individual or a group that allows others to categorise them and perhaps treat them accordingly

  (c) A prejudiced image of those that possess differing cultural, social and political values to those of others

  (d) The result of the process of assigning perceived negative attributes to particular individuals or groups

  (e) The image we have of others in relation to our own standing within our own social group

9 Which of the following are the three **overarching reasons** why prejudice arises?

  (a) Individual, interpersonal and inter-group (social) factors

  (b) Cultural, political and social factors

  (c) Innate, behavioural (learned) and experiential factors

  (d) Emotional, physical and by social group factors

  (e) Gender, race and religion factors

10 Which quality in the passage is **not** used to characterise a stereotype?

  (a) negative

  (b) positive

  (c) necessary

  (d) emotional

  (e) prejudicial

Passage 4: action for road safety

In March the United Nations General Assembly proclaimed the UN Decade of Action for Road Safety. The goal of the Decade, endorsed by more than 100 governments, is to 'stabilise and then reduce' global road death and injury. There's the chance, according to leading road safety experts, to save five million lives and prevent fifty million serious injuries in the next 10 years.

According to some projections, in five years' time, in the 5–14 year olds age group, road accidents will be a greater health burden on children than either malaria or tuberculosis or HIV/AIDS. It is only when you put it in that context that the decision-makers and indeed the public begin to realize that this is not a minor problem.

Some people would argue that poor countries just can't afford to make the investments that would be needed to achieve what you want to see in road safety. One of the bitter ironies of development economics is that developments are often seen through the eyes of the privileged and the rich. In a country like Kenya, most of the people do not own a car. Most people walk long distances either to a Matatu stand, the taxi stands or to public transport, inadequate as it is.

A survey by the Fédération Internationale de l'Automobile (FIA) Foundation found that road accidents claim the lives of 3,500 every day, 3,000 of which are people in poor countries. This will rise to more than 5,700 a day in 10 years' time unless governments act. Unlike deadly diseases, road traffic injuries were 'conspicuous' by their absence from the international development agenda.

The increase in road fatalities in developing countries is partly due to the increased level of traffic. Along with this is that these countries rarely separate traffic streams from pedestrians or build raised kerbs. Another factor was that often well-meaning safety legislation had little effect in countries where seat belts were rarely worn, there was no obligation for motorcyclists to wear crash helmets, air bags were not being fitted in new cars, and where no one could anticipate with any certainty the behaviour of the average road user.

On sub-Sahara African highways the projected deaths are set to double, while in Europe they will fall by 36% in the next 10 years. In Ethiopia figures show 100 people were killed for every 10,000 cars. The comparable ratio for Japan is one death for every 10,000 cars.

It is suggested that rich countries have been complicit in this slaughter. While donors such as the World Bank, wealthy nations and rising powers such as China have poured money into roads to help with the transport of commodities to ports, the construction has been done without 'specific legislative targets for reducing fatalities and injuries'. Road deaths and injuries are not accidents but caused by the criminal neglect of road safety; governments and aid donors need to stop measuring the success of their policies in kilometres of roads, and start thinking about the safety of road users.

Passage: 4 action for road safety questions

11 Which of the following is intended as the **significant** point about road death?

(a) Road death will in time kill more children than major illnesses

(b) The largest percentage of road death occurs in poor countries

(c) The reduction of road death needs to be given as much priority as the development of new roads

(d) The poor countries do not enforce road safety measures

(e) Countries place more value on the sale of commodities and wealth growth than on life

12 Which of the following words is being used as a **criticism** in the passage?

(a) 'burden'

(b) 'ironies'

(c) 'ratio'

(d) 'well-meaning'

(e) 'measuring'

13 Which of the following is **implied** but **not stated?**

(a) Economic development has a price

(b) Volume of traffic is not related to the number of deaths

(c) Wealth is more important than life

(d) The international development agenda is biased

(e) Pedestrian areas reduce accidents

14 The **tone** of the writing in the first two paragraphs is designed to do which of the following?

(a) inform

(b) educate

(c) upset

(d) provoke

(e) shock

Passage 5: democracy

There is no single theory of democracy; only theories. Beyond the broad commitment to rule by the majority, democracy involves a set of contentious debates concerning the proper function and scope of power, equality, freedom, justice and interests. Classical, modern and contemporary commentators have been concerned with the deep and diverse roots of the democratic ideal, and provide for ways of thinking about how some contemporary theories build on different traditions of democratic theorizing.

Aristotle's view of democratic government does not mesh with most contemporary theories, such as Robert Dahl's pluralism, nor with the views of feminist writers like Anne Phillips or the post-modern orientation of William Connolly. For some, democracy is about protecting freedom from a government that favours rulers and their friends at the expense of the rest. For others, democracy should reflect the interests of citizens and remain responsive to the concerns of organized groups. Alternate democratic voices call for a more active government to address the problems of the most vulnerable citizens. Still others see obstacles to full democratic citizenship coming not only from the state but located throughout society in ways which diminish the egalitarian principle of democratic politics and which, therefore, need to be resisted.

Take the idea of citizenship. Aristotle ties it to the ownership of private property, but virtually all twentieth century democratic theorists deny the connection. Friedrich Hayek thinks democratic citizens should most value their freedom and use their democratic resources to resist intervention by the state in what should be private. Yet this position is rejected by most other contemporary theorists who, for all of their different ideas about where to draw the line between the public and private, generally give the democratic state greater latitude than Hayek.

One of the most contentious issues has to do with the role of interests in a democracy. Socrates puts the negative case about interests in poignant and blunt terms. His Republic is built around a theory of justice where all of the parts cohere harmoniously. But the search for justice is undermined when those who rule put their interests ahead of the good of the whole. For this reason, Socrates wants his philosopher kings and queens to do without family (that is, spouses and children of their own) and without private property. As he understands matters, such attachments distract rulers from searching for justice and so, he reasons, interests need to be banished from politics. Even though civic republicans reject Socrates' strictures regarding the family and property, they retain his hostility to interests as a driving force in politics. And so do many other contemporary critics of liberal democratic practice.

Passage 5: democracy questions

15 What comes closest to the **meaning** of 'latitude' as used in the third paragraph?

   (a) scope

   (b) licence

   (c) parallel

   (d) initiative

   (e) freedom

16 Which of the following provides the best **definition** of the word 'democracy' as used in this passage?

   (a) A popular government

   (b) A political philosophy

   (c) A republic

   (d) A political belief

   (e) A commonwealth

17 What is the **main** argument made by Friedrich Hayek in relation to democracy?

   (a) What is private should remain so

   (b) People should resist state intervention

   (c) Freedom comes at a price

   (d) Freedom is of the highest value

   (e) Privacy is of the highest value

18 What comes closest to Socrates' **meaning** of the phrase 'interests need to be banished from politics'?

   (a) Without attachments and personal wealth

   (b) Without spouses and children

   (c) Without a spouse, children and private property

   (d) Without wealth and private property

   (e) Without family and private property

Passage 6: animals and morality

Animals exist on the borderline of our moral concepts; the result is that we sometimes find ourselves according them a strong moral status, while at other times denying them any kind of moral status at all.

Philosophical thinking on the moral standing of animals is diverse and one of the general categories of thinking relates to what are referred to as 'indirect theories'. These theories deny animals' moral status or equal consideration with humans due to a lack of consciousness, reason, or autonomy. Aristotle considered that there is a natural hierarchy of living beings. Human beings are superior to animals because human beings have the capacity for using reason to guide their conduct, while animals lack this ability and must instead rely on instinct.

St Thomas Aquinas believed that if a being cannot direct its own actions then others must do so; these sorts of beings are merely instruments. Instruments exist for the sake of people that use them, not for their own sake.

Immanuel Kant developed a highly influential moral theory. Morally permissible actions are those actions that could be willed by all rational individuals in the circumstances. The important part of his conception for the moral status of animals is his reliance on the notion of willing. While both animals and human beings have desires that can compel them to action, only human beings are capable of standing back from their desires and choosing which course of action to take. This ability is manifested by our wills. Since animals lack this ability, they lack a will, and therefore are not autonomous. According to Kant, the only thing with any intrinsic value is a good will. Since animals have no wills at all, they cannot have good wills; they therefore do not have any intrinsic value.

One of the clearest and most forceful denials of animal consciousness is developed by René Descartes, who argues that animals are automata that might act as if they are conscious, but really are not so – Descartes believed that all of animal behaviour could be explained in purely mechanistic terms, and that no reference to conscious episodes was required for such an explanation. Relying on the principle of parsimony in scientific explanation (commonly referred to as Occam's Razor) Descartes preferred to explain animal behaviour by relying on the simplest possible explanation of their behaviour. Since it is possible to explain animal behaviour without reference to inner episodes of awareness, doing so is simpler than relying on the assumption that animals are conscious, and is therefore the preferred explanation.

Philosophical thinkers such as Peter Singer, in supporting moral equity theories, would argue that if we were to rely on a humans rationality, autonomy and the ability to act morally, as the basis of determining moral status, then we would justify a kind of discrimination against certain human beings that is structurally analogous to such practices as racism and sexism. Tom Regan argues for animal rights by relying on the concept of inherent value. According to Regan, any being that is a subject-of-a-life is a being that has inherent value. A being that has inherent value is a being towards which we must show respect; in order to show respect to such a being, we cannot use it merely as a means to our ends. Instead, each such being must be treated as an end in itself. In other words, a being with inherent value has rights, and these rights act as trumps against the promotion of the overall good.

Passage 6: animals and morality questions

19 Which one of the following pair of traits is **not** descriptive of indirect theories?

(a) decision-making and autonomy

(b) rationality and discretion

(c) intrinsic value and consciousness

(d) inherent value and interdependence

(e) mechanistic and willing

20 Which one of the following statements comes **closest** to the criticism of indirect theories argued by Peter Singer?

(a) All life that can direct its own actions has inherent value irrespective of race or gender

(b) Indirect theories could be interpreted in a way that may expose human beings to discriminatory practices

(c) Humans' rationality, autonomy and ability to act morally cannot alone determine moral status

(d) The ability to choose a course of action should not determine the moral status of humans over animals

(e) There is no justification in denying animals moral status based on their lack of consciousness, reason, or autonomy

21 In relation to the passage, which one of the following statements **best describes** Occam's Razor?

(a) A principle that suggests we should tend towards simpler theories

(b) Science tends to prefer a more logical explanation

(c) The simplest hypothesis proposed as an explanation of phenomena is more likely to be the true one

(d) Selecting the competing hypothesis that makes the fewest new assumptions

(e) The world is actually simple and simple accounts are more likely than complex ones to be true

Passage 7: immigration cap

Employers have warned the government that the introduction of an immigration cap on skilled workers outside the EU will lead to major UK skills problems. The reason for an immigration cap comes at a time when new figures showed an unexpected 20% rise in net migration to Britain in the past 12 months.

Last year 196,000 people arrived in the UK, up from 163,000 the year before. However, this rise was fuelled mostly by 60% fewer Britons leaving the country to live abroad – down from 90,000 to 36,000. In addition there was a 3.7% rise in the number of overseas students coming to Britain. The total number of overseas students was 330,000 (out of a total of 2.3 million students in higher education), driven by a surge in students coming to the UK from India – up by more than 15%.

At the same time, the actual number of people coming to work in Britain has continued to decline. There was a fall of 14% in the past 12 months which included a 30% fall in new national insurance registrations by Poles and other eastern Europeans.

Britain has become much less attractive to migrants as a result of the recession and the weakened pound.

The government claim that the sharp fall in the number of work-related visas – down by 14% to 161,050 in the past 12 months – showed the points-based system was robust and working. However, employers argue that the reality is that training workers to plug the UK skills gap is a lengthy task. The abrupt introduction of a radical cap would therefore leave many employers with a bigger skills problem and tempt employers with global operations to offshore jobs, where they can find the skills.

The immigration cap on what is known as Tier 1 non-EU people – the category that allows highly skilled people to look for work or self-employment opportunities in the UK – will be cut from the present 13,000 per annum to 1,000. It is suggested that this will allow for 'exceptional people' such as sports stars and scientists to work in the UK.

The cap on Tier 2 non-EU people – the category of highly skilled people who already have job offers – will be cut by a fifth, from 28,000 a year down to 21,700.

Due to employers' concerns, concessions will include big global companies being allowed to continue to bring in non-EU workers under what is known as the Intra-Company Transfer (ICT) system. Where such workers remain in the UK for less than 12 months they are to be paid a salary of at least £24,000; for periods in excess of 12 months their salary must be at least £40,000. The ICT system will enable 22,500 non-EU workers to transfer each year.

A government spokesman said that there is also a need to look at the other routes by which people come into the country, maybe for education, for family reunion reasons and also, in particular, routes that lead to permanent settlement. Because hidden in these figures are two very big increases: one, of the number of students coming in, and the other, of the numbers of people settling here and gaining citizenship here.

Passage 7: immigration cap questions

22 What is the **main** reason for the increase in net migration to Britain?

   (a) The fall in new national insurance registrations by Poles and other Eastern Europeans

   (b) Tier 1 non-EU people looking for work or self-employment

   (c) A surge in students from overseas coming to the UK to study

   (d) Tier 2 non-EU people who already had job offers

   (e) Fewer Britons leaving the UK to live abroad

23 All of the statements below illustrate migration trends in the UK **except**:

   (a) The number of students from the Indian sub continent using higher education is increasing.

   (b) Non-EU workers especially those from Eastern European countries are decreasing.

   (c) An increase in the number of people deciding against leaving the UK to live abroad.

   (d) An increase in the number of highly skilled workers migrating to the UK under the ICT system.

   (e) The number of non-EU highly skilled people who have job offers will be reduced.

24 Which one of the following statements **best describes** what is being suggested by the last paragraph of the passage?

   (a) Immigrants are being allowed into the UK for the purposes of education outside the higher education sector without sufficient vigilance of any abuses

   (b) Foreign nationals are being allowed entry to the UK for the purposes of family reunions or other family matters that may need to be better policed

   (c) Migration to the UK, whether within employment controls or not, might be subject to abuse by people seeking permanent residence and citizenship

   (d) Another route into the UK may include illegal entry to the UK and further measures need to be considered in tackling this issue

(e) There is a hidden population of immigrants settling in the UK and controls need to counteract this problem

Passage 8: origins of the universe

The broadest definition of the universe was provided by Johannes Scotus Eriugena, a ninth century medieval philosopher who defined it as simply everything: everything that is created and everything that is not created. Time is not considered in Eriugena's definition; thus, his definition includes everything that exists, has existed and will exist, as well as everything that does not exist, has never existed and will never exist.

Historically, many models of the cosmos and its origin have been proposed, based on the then-available data and conceptions of the universe. Cosmologies and cosmogonies were based on narratives of gods acting in various ways. Theories of an impersonal universe governed by physical laws were first proposed by the Greeks and Indians. Over the centuries, improvements in astronomical observations and theories of motion and gravitation led to ever more accurate descriptions of the universe. The modern era of cosmology began with Albert Einstein's 1915 'General Theory of Relativity' which made it possible to quantitatively predict the origin, evolution, and conclusion of the universe as a whole. Most modern, accepted theories of cosmology are based on general relativity and, more specifically, the predicted Big Bang, however, still more careful measurements are required to determine which theory is correct.

Many cultures have stories describing the origin of the world, which may be roughly grouped into common types. In one type of story, the world is born from a 'world egg' primordial being coming into existence by 'hatching from an egg, e.g. the Chinese story of 'Oangu' or the Indian 'Brahmanda Purana'. In related stories, the creation idea is caused by a single entity emanating or producing something by him- or herself, as in Tibetan Buddhism, the ancient Greek story of 'Gaia' (Mother Earth), the Aztec goddess 'Coaticue', or the Genesis creation story. In another type of story, the world is created from the union of male and female deities, as in the Maori story of 'Rangi and Papa'. In other stories, the universe is created by crafting it from pre-existing materials, such as the corpse of a dead god – as from 'Tiamat' in the Babylonian epic 'Enuma Elish' or from the giant 'Ymir' in Norse mythology. In other stories, the universe emanates from fundamental principles, such as Brahman and Prakrti, or the yin and yang of the Tao.

The three major Abrahamic religions are, in order of appearance, Judaism, Christianity and Islam. They have been intertwined throughout their histories. They are considered inextricably linked to one another because of a 'family likeness' and a certain commonality in theology: all three are monotheistic (belief in the existence of one god), and conceive God to be a transcendent Creator-figure and the source of moral law. The sacred narratives of all three of these religions feature many of the same figures, histories and places in each, although they often present them with different roles, perspectives and meanings.

As of the early twenty-first century there were an estimated 3.8 billion followers of these three Abrahamic religions, It is estimated that 54% of the world's population consider themselves adherents of the Abrahamic religions, about 30% of other religions, and 16% are non-religious.

Passage 8: origins of the universe questions

25 Which one of the following statements is **not** part of Eriugena's definition of the universe?

(a) That which creates and is not created

(b) That which is created and creates

(c) That which is created and does not create

(d) That which neither is created nor creates

(e) That which creates the creation

26 What comes closest to the **main** argument in the paragraph that begins **'Historically, many models of the cosmos and its origin ... '**?

(a) Abrahamic faiths do not believe in Einstein's theory

(b) Cosmology is the study of the origins of humanity

(c) Einstein proved the physical origin and evolution of the universe

(d) Theories of physical laws seek to explain the origins of the universe

(e) Astronomy has advanced the theory of creation over evolution

27 Which of the following statements is true? Abrahamic religions:

(a) are the main religions in all countries across the world

(b) believe in the existence of one creator

(c) feature the same figures, histories and places

(d) do not believe in evolution

(e) are practised by over 50 per cent of the world's population.

28 In paragraph four of the passage what does the writer **mean** by the word 'transcendental'?

(a) outrageous

(b) supernatural

(c) nonsensical

(d) magnificent

(e) bizarre

Passage 9: *early years education*

The Reggio Emilia approach to early years education in northern Italy emphasises the joint endeavour between adults and children and children and children in creating an open environment of trust and wonder in which creativity is allowed to flourish naturally. Reciprocity and negotiation form part of the philosophical underpinning of Reggio Emilia and adults and children learn that collaboration is a powerful experience. The movement successfully promotes creativity by encouraging children's representational and expressive skills through a 'hundred languages' – the myriad ways in which children express themselves in a wider variety of media such as art, movement, language and music. Loris Malaguzzi, founder of the project, valued highly the benefits of a child-centred approach to learning. One research visitor, Leslie Abbott, noted several features of the Reggio Emilia pre-schools which make them particularly conducive to creative learning. She was particularly struck by the immediacy of the environment, in terms of the light and organisation of space and she gives the following description:

> 'Distinctive in all the … preschools is the piazza: the central meeting place where children from all around the school share their play and conversations together. The tetrahedron with the mirrored interior is often to be found there, with children sitting or standing inside it with their friends, looking at themselves, and many versions of themselves … mirrors proliferate in all the centres in keeping with the central philosophy of 'seeing oneself' and of constructing one's identity. Another distinctive feature … is the atelier, the art studio, where children work with the atelierista … the qualified artist who is a member of staff.'

> (Abbott and Nutbrown eds (2001) Experiencing Reggio Emilia: Open University Press)

Abbott reports that children's work adorns the buildings, showing the evolution of projects undertaken by groups of children and quotes Malaguzzi's words 'We place enormous value on the role of the environment as a motivating and animating force in creating spaces for relations, options, and emotional and cognitive situations that produce a sense of well-being and security'. Another visiting researcher, Katz, noted that 'no evidence was seen of all the children subjected to instruction at the same time, of having to create the same pictures or other art products – a common sight in our schools … ' By contrast with what we might find in many UK settings, children in the Reggio schools were able to carry out their own plans with confidence, and to take time to pursue their interests. Moreover, the adults also had unfailing confidence in the children's ability to succeed.

At present the early years education system in the UK works against those who learn kinaesthetically and visually and favours those who learn best through language and text. A system that encouraged and fostered creativity beyond that of the written word would, at the very least, give all children more options. At its best, it could revolutionise our understanding of what real learning is about!

Source: *Early Childhood Studies: Supporting Creativity* (eds Jenny Willan, Rod Parker-Rees and Jan Savage, Learning Matters Ltd 2007). © Jenny Willan, Rod Parker-Rees and Jan Savage. By kind permission of Learning Matters Ltd.

Passage 9: early years education questions

29 Which of the following phrases **best describes** the Reggio Emilia approach to education?

(a) Child-centred approach to learning

(b) Philosophy of 'seeing oneself' and of constructing one's identity

(c) Expressing skills through a 'hundred languages'

(d) Powerful experience of adults and children collaborating

(e) An open environment in which learning can flourish naturally

30 The **most important** fact that the writer seeks to convince the reader of is:

(a) A wide variety of media, such as art, movement, language and music, is crucial to allow children to express themselves

(b) Real learning is achieved in an education system that encourages and fosters a creative learning environment

(c) The UK does not encourage a child-centred approach to early years education

(d) Children who learn kinaesthetically and visually are better developed in their early years of education

(e) The role of the environment is crucial as a motivating and animating force in the promotion of the myriad ways of learning

31 Which one of the following statements could be substituted in place of Abbott and Nutbrown's observation **'The tetrahedron with the mirrored interior is often to be found there ...'** and still retain the same meaning?

(a) A triangular pyramid with a mirrored interior is often found in the piazza

(b) A light and spacious building with a mirrored interior is often found there

(c) A cylindrical structure with a mirrored interior is often found in the piazza

(d) A terraced construction with a mirrored interior is often found there

(e) An angular structure with a mirrored interior is often found in the piazza

32 In relation to the passage which one of the following statements about early years education is correct?

(a) In the UK adults have little confidence in their early years children's ability to succeed

(b) Reggio Emilia early years children are far more developed in constructing their own identity than children in the UK

(c) In the UK there is minimal support for early years children who learn by actually carrying out a physical activity

(d) Reggio Emilia children have a better relationship with adults than children in the UK

(e) In the UK early years children do not have qualified artists who are members of staff

Passage 10: the aging process

Three of the theories that account for the processes involved in physical aging are, wear and tear theory, cellular theory, and immunity theory. Klatz and Goldman (1997) explain that the 'wear and tear' theory is based on the assumption that living organisms are like machines. It proposes that just as machines such as cars 'wear out' with use and time, each human's physiology is affected in a similar manner. The theory runs that over time the body accumulates damage from external factors, such as pollution, as well as interior factors, such as poor diet. By the time old age is reached the body is vulnerable to the ultimate factor that leads to the individual's death.

James (1995) explains that 'cellular theory' investigates how disease arises from micro-organisms within the cell of the body. In particular, the theory is concerned with the ways in which errors in cell division occurring throughout life contribute to the degenerative conditions we see in later years. For example, an 'error' during the process of cell division could produce two faulty cells, which could then divide to form four faulty cells, dividing again to produce eight and so on, eventually impairing a function of part of the body. A second area of interest in cellular theory is the accumulation of toxic substances within the body as it develops into late adulthood. There are two particular explanations of aging that fall within this category, one involving changes in the body's ability to get rid of metabolic waste and the other relating to changes in what are known as 'collagens'. Some substances, such as 'lipofuscin', begin to build up in the body with advancing age. Collagen fibres are found in the body, particularly in muscles, joints and bones and age-related changes in these fibres can be seen in various external signs of aging, such as wrinkling of the skin, sagging muscles and a tendency for slower healing of cuts and wounds.

Metchnikoff (2000) popularised 'immunity theory' that is explained at a physiological rather than a cellular level. This approach suggests that changes occurring in the body's immune system will eventually result in physical degeneration. With age the immune system becomes less efficient so there is an increased chance that harmful cells will not be killed off and these cells can cause damage to the body leading to degeneration. The first strand of immunity theory is based on the assumption that the immune system is unable to recognise slight deviations in faults in molecular structure and cell characteristics. This means that cells that have undergone mutation and would normally have been destroyed by the immune system are no longer recognised and are allowed to grow and develop, impacting on the health of the body. A second aspect of the theory suggests that even though the immune system can recognise these deviations, it is not able to produce enough antibodies to destroy them. A further variation of the immune theory, the 'auto-immune theory', sees aging as resulting from the development of antibodies within the body that destroy not only abnormal cells but also those that are normal and healthy, resulting in the auto-immune antibodies working in a self-destructive way. Several versions of the immune theory exist each focussing on a different level of functioning within the immune system as a whole.

Source: *Applied Psychology for Social Work: Psychology and old age* (by Ewan Ingleby, Learning Matters Ltd, 2006). © Ewan Ingleby. By kind permission of Learning Matters Ltd

Passage 10: the aging process questions

33 Which one of the following statements does **not** introduce a new argument?

(a) The condition of the blood is at the core of the immune system

(b) What a person eats can damage their physiology

(c) Changes in hormones control aging

(d) Positive thinking can extend human life

(e) Genetics may determine the length of human life

34 Which, if any, of the three theories would account for psychological degeneration during the aging process?

(a) None of the theories

(b) Wear and tear theory

(c) Cellular theory

(d) Immunity theory

(e) All of the theories

35 What do 'cellular theory' and 'immunity theory' have in common?

(a) Associated with errors in cell division

(b) Explain the theories of aging at a physiological level

(c) Account for the changes within the human body as people age

(d) Antibodies are unable to destroy toxic cells

(e) Cell impairment works in a self-destructive way

Passage 11: taxonomy of charities

An advisor to some of the country's biggest philanthropists has suggested that charities should be ranked according to their benefit to society to discourage ill-informed giving. Potential donors should have access to a 'taxonomy' of charities that classifies the most and least worthwhile causes.

The proposal has proved controversial among charity bosses, many of whom rely on donors who feel they are 'repaying' a benefit they have directly had from the charity or who have personal ties to a cause. The leader of the Association of Chief Executives of Voluntary Organisations branded the concept as dangerous, and the chief executive of the Charities Aid Foundation responded that giving was 'about our vulnerabilities' and a matter of personal preference.

The 'taxonomy' of charities would provide a framework that catalogues charitable causes, and, ultimately, charities, according to their field of work. The fact that some public schools have charity status has caused considerable disquiet and reflects a belief held by many that some things are more clearly charitable and deserving than others. People often point to the fact that more money has been given to a donkey sanctuary than to the victimcs helped by a charity for abuse and violence against women.

There has been a decline in the number of people giving to charities. Ten years ago, 68% of the population gave to charities but the current figure has dropped to 54%. Britons gave £9.9bn last year, less than 1% of the national income.

Research in the United States, similar to studies in Britain, has shown that 23% of donors support charities that have directly benefited them, while 31% are casual givers or people who have personal ties to the cause. Just 14% of donors support causes where they think they can generate the most social good. It has been identified that almost two-thirds of donors do not research the charities they give to and those that do usually spend no more than a couple of hours.

It has been suggested that the 'taxonomy' of charities might include an index and a minimal system of prioritising needs and that something like Maslow's hierarchy of needs could be useful. This begins with basic needs such as food and water, rising through to safety, belonging, esteem and ending with self-actualisation (such as creativity).

Passage 11: taxonomy of charities questions

36 Which of the following does the writer present as **paradoxical?**

(a) Some public schools have charity status

(b) There has been a decline in charitable donations

(c) Donors do not research the charity they give to

(d) Charities should be ranked according to their benefit to society

(e) People have given more money to a donkey sanctuary than to a welfare charity

37 Based on the passage, which of the following would be the **main** priority of classification for the 'taxonomy of charities'?

(a) Merit

(b) Good cause

(c) Personal preference

(d) Beneficiary donors

(e) Social good

38 What is the voluntary sector's **main** objection to a 'taxonomy of charities'?

(a) People may donate to the bigger charities

(b) It may take away personal choice

(c) It may affect the decision-making of donors

(d) People may donate less to charities

(e) People may not donate to charities that have helped them

39 Which of the following is **not stated** in the passage?

(a) The number of Britons donating to charities is less now than ten years ago

(b) Social good is not the main priority of charitable donors

(c) Public schools can have charitable status

(d) The amount donated by Britons to charities was less last year than previous years

(e) Almost a quarter of those who donate to charity have a personal reason for doing so

Passage 12: critical reflection

When described in the literature critical reflection is usually referred to as the thinking activities engaged in to critically analyse and evaluate experiences, producing outcomes of new understandings and appreciations of the way we think and operate. The concept of self-awareness is always apparent, which allows the subjective element (feelings and emotions associated with a situation) to be analysed and evaluated at the same time. The consideration of external knowledge to provide a broad and current context may also be included.

Schön (1983, 1987) developed ideas around two main types of reflection in practice: 'reflection on action' – when we think back on something already done; and 'reflection in action' – when we think about what we are doing while we are doing it.

The processes involved differ for each type of situation. When a person is actively doing something they rarely have the time or opportunity to be consciously deliberative or analytical, and so the manner of their 'reflection' is likely to be much more holistic, intuitive and automatic in the latter situation (Van Manen, 1995), even though we may still take a step back to quickly review what is going on.

Reflection will produce a lot of thoughts, ideas, connections and insights into a person's learning and development. Maudsley and Scrivens (2000) argue that reflection in practice unites discussion of critical thinking with experiential learning.

Understanding new ideas can involve the reassessment of old perspectives that can be discomforting, whereas exploring the things that have gone right can affirm and help understanding of experience and knowledge in detail. But reflecting on all types of experiences (the negative and positive) can: allow greater awareness and expression of all types of learning and development; show enhanced understanding from why things did work as well as why they didn't; and provide a more positive ending for the negative experiences rather than just leaving things as they were and allow a proper and full recognition of the good experiences and one's strengths.

However, placing oneself at the centre of an event or experience can lead to a preoccupation with the self that can border on self-absorption. To avoid this happening, a person needs to ensure that their reflection turns outwards as well, i.e. onto practice values, principles, traditions and the wider context relevant to the issue.

Source: *Critical Thinking for Social Work: Critical Reflection* (by Keith Brown and Lynne Rutter, Learning Matters Ltd 2006). © Keith Brown and Lynne Rutter. By kind permission of Learning Matters Ltd.

Passage 12: critical reflection questions

40 Which one of the following sentences serves **to develop** the information contained in paragraph five of the passage?

   (a) Reflection allows for the critical analysis and evaluation of both positive and negative experiences

   (b) Be aware that overly reflecting on negative experiences can cause anxiety and defensiveness

   (c) In experiential learning, the learner changes from an active participant in an experience to a reflector

   (d) The development of the self as a critical practitioner is essential

   (e) In practice critical thinking and learning are essential when debating reflection

41 Which one of these phrases **best** sums up the idea of 'critical reflection'?

   (a) The processes of being consciously deliberative or analytical

   (b) The ability to reflect, to be self-aware and to question

   (c) The concept of self-awareness in evaluating skills and beliefs

   (d) The processes involved in developing personal ability

   (e) Being self-aware, analysing and evaluating practical experiences

42 In paragraph three of the passage which one of the following words does **not** mean 'consciously deliberative'?

   (a) Intuitive

   (b) Planned

   (c) Premeditated

   (d) Intentional

   (e) Calculated

10. LNAT® *practice test answers*

Below are the correct answers to the 42 multiple-choice questions. A full explanation of the rationale for both the correct and incorrect answers follows in the next section of this chapter.

Question	Answer	Question	Answer
1	(d)	22	(e)
2	(a)	23	(d)
3	(b)	24	(c)
4	(e)	25	(e)
5	(c)	26	(d)
6	(b)	27	(b)
7	(d)	28	(d)
8	(b)	29	(a)
9	(a)	30	(b)
10	(e)	31	(a)
11	(c)	32	(c)
12	(d)	33	(b)
13	(c)	34	(e)
14	(e)	35	(c)
15	(a)	36	(e)
16	(b)	37	(a)
17	(d)	38	(c)
18	(c)	39	(d)
19	(d)	40	(b)
20	(b)	41	(e)
21	(a)	42	(a)

Passage 1: Oxbridge Prejudice?

These questions are related to the passage on page 37.

1   This passage is an extract from a speech. To whom do you think the speech was addressed?

(a) Oxbridge lecturers

(b) Student applicants

(c) Parents

(d) Politicians

(e) Commission for Racial Equality

Question 1: answer and rationale

The question is asking you to **whom** do you think the speech was addressed. In order to answer this question you will need to examine the passage very carefully, to make an informed judgment. The highlighted statement and rationale is correct:

(a) Oxbridge lecturers

This is an incorrect answer as it is unlikely that a speech that is suggesting that Oxford and Cambridge may be racially prejudiced in their selection procedures would be delivered to their lecturers.

(b) Student applicants

This is an incorrect answer as it would be an inappropriate speech to make to student applicants who are considering their options.

(c) Parents

This is an incorrect answer as it is unlikely that a speech that is suggesting that Oxford and Cambridge may be racially prejudiced in their selection procedures would be delivered to parents of potential applicants.

(d) Politicians

This is the correct answer as the fourth paragraph refers to 'a fellow Labour MP' which indicates that the speech is being delivered by another Labour MP as part of a parliamentary debate.

(e) Commission for Racial Equality

This is an incorrect answer as it is unlikely that a politician would present such material to this group who should already be well informed of the suggested racial prejudice at Oxford and Cambridge.

2 Which one of the following is an **assertion of fact** rather than **opinion**?

(a) 'An Oxford spokesman informed me'

(b) 'where variations exist this is due to supply of applications and demand by subject'

(c) 'the figures are too low for the variation between colleges to be statistically significant'

(d) 'poor attainment at school level narrows the pool'

(e) 'black candidates are more likely to apply to elite universities'

Question 2: *answer and rationale*

The question is asking you which one of the following is an **assertion of fact** rather than **opinion**. A **fact** is something that exists whereas an **opinion** means a judgment or belief that is not founded on certainty or proof. In order to answer this question you will need to examine the passage very carefully. The highlighted statement and rationale is correct:

(a) 'An Oxford spokesman informed me'

This is the correct answer as it is an assertion of the fact that an Oxford spokesman passed on information which may in itself be the opinion of that person but the act actually happened.

(b) 'where variations exist this is due to supply of applications and demand by subject'

This is an incorrect answer as it is the opinion of the Oxford spokesman which does not appear to be supported by the figures presented in the passage.

(c) 'the figures are too low for the variation between colleges to be statistically significant'

This is an incorrect answer as it is a statement made by Oxford without the detail of sample sizes and other statistical evidence to support the statement.

(d) 'poor attainment at school level narrows the pool'

This is an incorrect answer as it is an opinion of the most selective universities without the data to support it.

(e) 'black candidates are more likely to apply to elite universities'

This is an incorrect answer as it is an opinion of the most selective universities without the data to support it.

3   Which of the following does the writer **imply** but not **state**?

   (a) Black students are less intelligent compared to white students

   (b) That Oxford and Cambridge select on the basis of class as well as attainment

   (c) Working-class students are still under-represented in British universities

   (d) White students are over five times more successful than black students at Newnham College, Cambridge

   (e) Research-intensive universities are not attractive to working-class students

Question 3: *answer and rationale*

The question is asking you to identify which statement is **implied** but not directly **stated** by the writer but does follow logically from statements made in the passage. Again you are looking for which of the options is true or false (correct or incorrect) given the question. There are two types of statements that would be incorrect. The first type of potential answer would be one where the proposition is directly stated as the question asks you to identify issues, which are not directly stated. It follows that anything that is explicit (actually stated) must be incorrect in the light of the instruction you have been given in this particular question. The highlighted statement and rationale is correct:

(a) Black students are less intelligent compared with white students

   This is an incorrect answer as it is not implied or indeed stated. The writer only comments on the performance evidence and does not make any assertions as to the cause of differential performance. In addition this statement is offensive.

(b) That Oxford and Cambridge select on the basis of class as well as attainment

   This is the correct answer as it can be implied by the information provided by the writer. The evidence provided in each paragraph supports this implication, in particular the deviation from the mean in terms of the social profile of these two universities.

(c) Working-class students are still under-represented in British universities

   This is an incorrect answer as it is clearly stated that this is the case, for example: 'It is no secret that there aren't huge numbers of students from working-class backgrounds' and the quoted statistic that an average of 64.5 per cent of the student body in British universities is drawn from the top three socio-economic groups.

(d) White students are over five times more successful than black students at Newnham College, Cambridge

   This is an incorrect answer as it is clearly stated in the passage. The penultimate paragraph states that the success rate at this college for white students is 67 per cent compared with 13 per cent for black students. 67 per cent is more than five times greater than 13 per cent therefore it is stated.

(e) Research-intensive universities are not attractive to working-class students

This is an incorrect answer as it is not implied in the passage. The first paragraph states: 'Eight of the 10 universities with the lowest proportions of working-class students were in the prestigious Russell Group of research-intensive universities.' However, that statement does not imply that working-class students are not attracted to these universities.

4   It might be suggested from the passage that the following provide evidence of prejudice at Oxbridge institutions, **except**:

(a) '...21 of their colleges made no offers to black students last year.'

(b) '...there aren't huge numbers of students from working-class backgrounds...'

(c) '...of more than 1,500 academic and lab staff at Cambridge, none are black.'

(d) '...white candidates were three and a half times more successful than black candidates over an 11-year period.'

(e) '...where variations exist this is due to supply of applications and demand by subject.'

Question 4: answer and rationale

The question is asking you to identify which one of the statements **is not** quoted by the writer as a suggested reason for prejudice. In order to answer this question you will need to examine each of the statements very carefully to ascertain whether or not they suggest a reason for prejudice. The highlighted statement and rationale is correct:

(a) '...21 of their colleges made no offers to black students last year.'

This is an incorrect answer as it is one of the claims being made in the passage that 21 of the Oxford and Cambridge colleges made no offers to black students in the last year, providing circumstantial evidence of prejudice against black applicants.

(b) '...there aren't huge numbers of students from working-class backgrounds...'

This is an incorrect answer as it is quoted in the passage that 8 out of 10 of the Russell Group of universities has the lowest proportions of working-class students that provides circumstantial evidence of prejudice against applicants from working-class backgrounds.

(c) '...of more than 1,500 academic and lab staff at Cambridge, none are black.'

This is an incorrect answer as the passage actually states that none of 1,500 academic lab staff at Cambridge are black and this again provides circumstantial evidence of prejudice when employing black people as academic and lab staff.

(d) '...white candidates were three and a half times more successful than black candidates over an 11-year period.'

This is an incorrect answer as the Freedom of Information data in the passage states that '...Jesus College white candidates were three and a half times more successful than black candidates over an 11-year period.' This provides circumstantial evidence of prejudice against black applicants.

(e) '...where variations exist this is due to supply of applications and demand by subject.'

This is the correct answer as it states in the passage 'An Oxford spokesman informed me that black students apply disproportionately for the most oversubscribed subjects, contributing to a lower than average success rate for the group as a whole.' This is essentially presented as evidence to contradict an allegation of prejudice on the grounds of, in this instance, colour, and therefore is the exception.

Passage 2: Media technologies and children

These questions are related to the passage on page 39.

5   According to the passage what is the **main disadvantage** of media technology?

(a) Young children are the victims of media technology

(b) Media technology encourages violence

(c) Media technology can be damaging to young people

(d) Media technology is hypnotic

(e) Media technology is inferior to books

Question 5: answer and rationale

The question is asking you to identify which one of the statements is the **main disadvantage** of media technology. It does not suggest that other disadvantages will not be present. This is an evaluation as to whether the options provided are the main disadvantage or not, in other words, whether they are true or false in relation to the question. In order to address this question it is necessary to read the passage thoroughly in order to follow the ideas and the structure of the argument to reach a conclusion as to which option is the fundamental disadvantage of media technology. The highlighted statement and rationale is correct:

(a) Young children are the victims of media technology

This is an incorrect answer. It is quoted in the first paragraph as one side of the argument against media technology but it does not encompass all the disadvantages.

(b) Media technology encourages violence

This is an incorrect answer. It is quoted in the first paragraph as one side of the argument that media technology encourages children to indulge in violent computer games but that is not to say it encourages violence.

(c) Media technology can be damaging to young people

This is the correct answer as it encompasses all the points raised in the passage about the potential downside of technology, i.e. the exposure to violent games, the overexposure to television, the hypnotic power of the screen and the value of such 'entertainment' both culturally and morally.

(d) Media technology is hypnotic

This is an incorrect answer. It is quoted in the first paragraph as one side of the argument against media technology but it does not encompass all the disadvantages.

(e) Media technology is inferior to books

This is an incorrect answer as no comparison is made in the passage between the use of media technology and books to aid creative development. The evidence quoted in the last three paragraphs supports the view that television viewing in the right context can be a positive aid to language development and creative writing.

6   Which is the **most significant** point of the quoted research?

(a) Media technology helps children develop language and writing skills

(b) Skills developed through the use of media technology are transferable

(c) Children taught using media technology are more creative in their written work

(d) The vocabulary of children can be increased by television viewing

(e) Children respond well to media technology

Question 6: answer and rationale

The question is asking you to identify which one of the statements is the **most significant** point of the quoted research. It does not suggest that other significant points will not be present. This is an evaluation as to whether the options provided are the most significant or not, in other words, whether they are true or false in relation to the question. In order to address this question it is necessary to read the passage thoroughly in order to follow the ideas and the structure of the argument to reach a conclusion as to which option is the most significant point of the quoted research. The highlighted statement and rationale is correct:

(a) Media technology helps children develop language and writing skills

This statement is an incorrect answer as it does not totally encompass the major finding from the quoted research.

(b) Skills developed through the use of media technology are transferable

This is the correct answer as the finding that skills developed through the use of media technology can be transferred to the written word has implications for the transfer of other skills or qualities in other subject areas.

(c) Children taught using media technology are more creative in their written work

This is an incorrect answer. Even though it is one of the findings of the research it is narrow in terms of the overall impact media technologies may have.

(d) The vocabulary of children can be increased by television viewing

This is an incorrect answer. Even though it is one of the findings of the research it is only one of the points that is quoted.

(e) Children respond well to media technology

This is an incorrect answer. It could be concluded from the passage that this is the case but a positive response to media technology does not in itself suggest any benefits in terms of skills development.

7   What is the **main** purpose of this passage?

   (a) To promote the use of media technology in schools

   (b) To drag education into the twenty-first century

   (c) To quote the pros and cons of media technology

   (d) To inform teachers of the potential benefits from the use of media technology

   (e) To support the financial investment that has been made in technology within schools

Question 7: answer and rationale

The question is asking you to identify which one of the statements is the **main** purpose of the passage. It does not suggest that a number of purposes will not be present. This is an evaluation as to whether the options provided are the main purpose or not, in other words, whether they are true or false in relation to the question. In order to address this question it is necessary to read the passage thoroughly in order to follow the ideas and the structure of the argument to reach a conclusion as to which option is the main purpose of the passage. The passage may contain several points that are relevant to the purpose of the passage as they help to build up a body of evidence. Therefore, it is important to examine the structure of the argument as this may indicate what the main purpose is. The highlighted statement and rationale is correct:

(a) To promote the use of media technology in schools

This is an incorrect answer as it can be assumed that the majority of schools do promote the use of media technology where it is appropriate.

(b) To drag education into the twenty-first century

This is an incorrect answer as it is a very sweeping statement and would therefore be a poor option.

(c) To quote the pros and cons of media technology

This is an incorrect answer as some of the pros and cons are quoted as part of the lead-in to the quoted research and are not the main point of the passage.

(d) To inform teachers of the potential benefits from the use of media technology

This is the correct answer as the passage has been written to inform the reader (most likely teachers) of the potential benefits that the use of media technology could have in their classroom.

(e) To support the financial investment that has been made in technology within schools

This is an incorrect answer as it would be a very cynical view of the reason for the passage.

Passage 3: Stereotyping

These questions are related to the passage on page 41.

8   Which of the following phrases **best defines** a stereotype?

(a) An image or conception of others that is shared by all members of a social group

(b) A set of generalisations about an individual or a group that allows others to categorise them and perhaps treat them accordingly

(c) A prejudiced image of those that possess differing cultural, social and political values to those of others

(d) The result of the process of assigning perceived negative attributes to particular individuals or groups

(e) The image we have of others in relation to our own standing within our own social group

Question 8: *answer and rationale*

The question is asking you to identify the statement that provides the **best definition** of the word 'stereotype'. The answer will obviously be contained within the passage but it may be that more than one statement has some relationship to the answer. You are looking for the statement that most closely accounts for or describes 'stereotype'. The highlighted statement and rationale is correct:

(a) An image or conception of others that is shared by all members of a social group

This is an incorrect answer as it forms only a part of the definition of a stereotype. It is clear from the passage that the phrase 'stereotype' is a complex social concept that has many facets and connotations.

(b) A set of generalisations about an individual or a group that allows others to categorise them and perhaps treat them accordingly

This is the correct answer in that it best describes the meaning of 'stereotype' in relation to the whole passage. The passage introduces a range of definitions from various researchers and also states common or popular beliefs, which range from being individualistic to broader socially held views. This statement would encapsulate the main tenet of the passage.

(c) A prejudiced image of those that possess differing cultural, social and political values to those of others

This is an incorrect answer as the second paragraph states: 'Stereotyping in itself is not necessarily negative. It is something that all of us engage in to form our views of the world.' The passage then does proceed to say that stereotyping is the cause of many prejudicial attitudes but that is not to say that all stereotyping is based on a prejudiced image.

(d) The result of the process of assigning perceived negative attributes to particular individuals or groups

This is an incorrect answer as the second paragraph states: 'Stereotyping in itself is not necessarily negative.' It is clear from the passage that a stereotype could be based on either perceived negative or positive attributes of an individual or a group.

(e) The image we have of others in relation to our own standing within our own social group

This is an incorrect answer. The statement is based on an individualistic view of a stereotype in relation to one's own standing within their own social group. It does not encompass the group dynamic which may influence an individual's perspective.

9 Which of the following are the three **overarching reasons** why prejudice arises?

(a) Individual, interpersonal and inter-group (social) factors

(b) Cultural, political and social factors

(c) Innate, behavioural (learned) and experiential factors

(d) Emotional, physical and by social group factors

(e) Gender, race and religion factors

Question 9: answer and rationale

The question is asking you to identify the **three overarching reasons** why prejudice arises. The three reasons will obviously be contained within the passage but more than one of the statements may have some relationship to the answer. By carefully reading the passage you need to identify the most appropriate three overarching reasons why prejudice arises. The highlighted statement and rationale is correct:

(a) Individual, interpersonal and inter-group (social) factors

This is the correct answer as it includes the overarching reasons why prejudice arises. The passage quotes research and views which relate to individual, interpersonal and inter-group (social factors) which may result in prejudicial attitudes.

(b) Cultural, political and social factors

This is an incorrect answer as the reasons are too specific and not broad enough to include all the arguments put forward in the passage. Prejudicial attitudes can of course stem from cultural, political and social beliefs and examples are given in the passage, but they are not the overarching reasons.

(c) Innate, behavioural (learned) and experiential factors

This is an incorrect answer as the reasons given are more related to the individual level, in particular innate tendencies. Learned behaviour and experiences may, in part, be at the group level and all of these reasons may be the source of some prejudices but this option is not the best choice of answer.

(d) Emotional, physical and by social group factors

This is an incorrect answer as the reasons given are based on the model quoted in the last paragraph which was first posited by Albert Bandura (1977). This, therefore, is too narrow to be the correct answer.

(e) Gender, race and religion factors

This is an incorrect answer as the reasons given are based on very specific sources of potential prejudices. The passage quotes research that relates directly to gender and race and indirectly quotes an example of possible prejudicial attitudes relating to religion in the third paragraph, 'prejudice arises against other people when we realise that they hold different, contradictory views to our own'. That being said, the reasons are not the overarching reasons asked for.

10 Which quality in the passage is **not** used to characterise a stereotype?

(a) negative

(b) positive

(c) necessary

(d) emotional

(e) prejudicial

Question 10: *answer and rationale*

The question is asking you to identify which quality is **not** used in the passage to characterise a stereotype. This seems reasonably straightforward and should be achieved by a process of elimination, i.e. determining which one of the words has not been used. In order to answer this question you will need to examine the passage very carefully. The highlighted statement and rationale is correct:

(a) negative

This is an incorrect answer as the second paragraph clearly states, 'Stereotyping in itself is not necessarily negative', which also implies that it can be negative. In addition the paragraph states, 'the prejudicial attitude is the process of labelling negative attributes'.

(b) positive

This is an incorrect answer as the second paragraph clearly states, 'Stereotyping in itself is not necessarily negative', which by definition means that it can be positive.

(c) necessary

This is an incorrect answer as the second paragraph clearly states, 'It is something that all of us engage in to form our views of the world'; therefore, it must be necessary.

(d) emotional

This is an incorrect answer as the last paragraph emphasises that the sharing of emotional bonds can reinforce prejudicial attitudes, therefore stereotypes can be emotionally driven.

(e) prejudicial

This is the correct answer as the passage does not state that a stereotype in itself is prejudicial; this quality is applied to the attitudes that may result from stereotyping.

Passage 4: action for road safety

These questions are related to the passage on page 43.

11 Which of the following is intended as the **significant** point about road death?

(a) Road death will in time kill more children than major illnesses

(b) The largest percentage of road death occurs in poor countries

(c) The reduction of road death needs to be given as much priority as the development of new roads

(d) The poor countries do not enforce road safety measures

(e) Countries place more value on the sale of commodities and wealth growth than on life

Question 11: answer and rationale

The question is asking you to identify which one of the statements is the **significant** point about road death. It does not suggest that other significant points will not be present. This is an evaluation as to whether the options provided are the most significant or not, in other words, whether they are true or false in relation to the question. In order to address this question it is necessary to read the passage thoroughly in order to follow the ideas and the structure of the argument to reach a conclusion as to which option is the most significant point about road death. The highlighted statement and rationale is correct:

(a) Road death will in time kill more children than major illnesses

This is an incorrect answer as it is not the significant point about the main theme of the passage. It is stated in the passage that 'road accidents will be a greater health burden … ' and this would imply that there will be more deaths but the statement only contributes to the significant point being made.

(b) The largest percentage of road death occurs in poor countries

This is an incorrect answer as it is not the significant point about the main tenet of the passage. It is stated in the passage that 'road accidents claim the lives of 3,500 every day, 3,000 of which are people in poor countries' but the statement only contributes to the significant point being made.

(c) The reduction of road death needs to be given as much priority as the development of new roads

This is the correct answer. It makes the significant point that road safety needs to be given as much priority as the commercial aspects of development, which is the main tenet of 'Action for Road Safety'.

(d) The poor countries do not enforce road safety measures

This is an incorrect answer as it is not the significant point about the main tenet of the passage. It is stated in the passage in relation to developing countries that 'safety legislation had little effect'. This supports the argument that more priority needs to be given to road safety but it is not the significant point being made.

(e) Countries place more value on the sale of commodities and wealth growth than on life

This is an incorrect answer as it is not the significant point about the main tenet of the passage. It could be inferred from the passage that this is the case but it is not the significant point that the passage is trying to put over to the reader.

12 Which of the following words is being used as a **criticism** in the passage?

(a) 'burden'

(b) 'ironies'

(c) 'ratio'

(d) 'well-meaning'

(e) 'measuring'

Question 12: *answer and rationale*

The question is asking you to identify which word in the passage is being used as a **criticism**. A criticism is a judgement of the merits and faults of a piece of work or actions of an individual or group by another. To criticize does not necessarily imply to find fault, but the word is often taken to mean the simple expression of an objection against prejudice or disapproval. The highlighted statement and rationale is correct:

(a) 'burden'

This is an incorrect answer as it is being used to emphasise and not criticise the impact road accidents will have on children's health.

(b) 'ironies'

This is an incorrect answer as it is being used to demonstrate the paradox of development economics and is not necessarily a criticism.

(c) 'ratio'

This is an incorrect answer. It is being used to demonstrate that road deaths in relation to the number of cars is 100 times higher in Ethiopia than Japan and is therefore being used as support and not criticism.

(d) 'well-meaning'

This is the correct answer as it is being used to criticise the apparent lip service that is being paid to safety legislation.

(e) 'measuring'

This in an incorrect answer as it is not the 'measuring' but the 'method' of measuring which is being used as a criticism in the passage.

13 Which of the following is **implied** but not **stated?**

(a) Economic development has a price

(b) Volume of traffic is not related to the number of deaths

(c) Wealth is more important than life

(d) The International development agenda is biased

(e) Pedestrian areas reduce accidents

Question 13: *answer and rationale*

The question is asking you to identify which statement is **implied** but not directly **stated** by the writer but does follow logically from statements made in the passage. Again you are looking for which of the options is true or false (correct or incorrect) given the question. There are two types of statements that would be incorrect. The first type of potential answer would be one where the proposition is directly stated as the question asks you to identify issues, which are not directly stated. It follows that anything that is explicit (actually stated) must be incorrect in the light of the instruction you have been given in this particular question. The highlighted statement and rationale is correct:

(a) Economic development has a price

This is an incorrect answer as it is clearly stated throughout the passage that the developing countries are paying a price by the increase in road fatalities and injuries.

(b) Volume of traffic is not related to the number of deaths

This is an incorrect answer as it is clearly stated in the passage that 'The increased in road fatalities in developing countries is partly due to the increased level of traffic.' Conversely, the comparison between the number of deaths in Ethiopia and Japan renders this statement untrue.

(c) Wealth is more important than life

This is the correct answer as it is implied that the developing countries and/or their financial backers are more interested in the commercial gains irrespective of the humanitarian issue of road safety.

(d) The international development agenda is biased

This is an incorrect answer as it is stated in the passage that 'Unlike deadly diseases, road traffic injuries were "conspicuous" by their absence from the international development agenda', which indicates a bias in their reporting.

(e) Pedestrian areas reduce accidents

This is an incorrect answer as it can be implied from the fifth paragraph that the separation of traffic streams and pedestrians would result in a reduction in accidents.

14 The **tone** of the writing in the first two paragraphs is designed to do which of the following?

(a) inform

(b) educate

(c) upset

(d) provoke

(e) shock

Question 14: *answer and rationale*

The question is asking you to identify what the **tone** of the passage is designed to do. Tone is a literary technique that encompasses the attitudes toward the subject and toward the audience implied in a literary work. Essentially you are trying to find which option best describes the tone of the writer in the first two paragraphs. The highlighted statement and rationale is correct:

(a) inform

This is an incorrect answer as the information is being used to ellicit a strong response that will hopefully result in action.

(b) educate

This is an incorrect answer as raising the awareness of readers will not necessarily instigate action.

(c) upset

This is an incorrect answer as the first two paragraphs are designed to emphasise the increasing problem of road safety and are not intended to 'upset' in an emotional sense.

(d) provoke

This is an incorrect answer as the content of the first two paragraphs could provoke reactions for and against the content of the passage.

(e) shock

> This is the correct answer as the projected statistics quoted in the opening two paragraphs are designed to 'shock' the reader by the enormity of the problem, thereby creating support for increased action for road safety.

Passage 5: democracy

These questions are related to the passage on page 45.

15 What comes closest to the **meaning** of 'latitude' as used in the third paragraph?

(a) scope

(b) licence

(c) parallel

(d) initiative

(e) freedom

Question 15: answer and rationale

The question is asking you to identify the word that has a similar **meaning** to 'latitude'. The answer will require you to establish the context in which the word 'latitude' is used within the third paragraph of the passage. It may be that more than one word has some relationship to the answer and you need to determine the one that comes closest to or best describes the word 'latitude'. The highlighted statement and rationale is correct:

(a) scope

> This is the correct answer as the word 'latitude' is being used to suggest that most other theorists give the democratic state more scope as to where to draw the line between the public and private.

(b) licence

> This is an incorrect answer as the word 'licence' means 'liberty of action on thought; freedom; and is more about giving permission, consent, approval, liberty, etc. Therefore this is not the closest meaning of 'latitude' in this context.

(c) parallel

> This is an incorrect answer as it is quite a different meaning of the word 'latitude'. This definition is more to do with position, analogy, symmetry, etc. and therefore is not the best option.

(d) initiative

This is an incorrect answer as it is more to do with making the first move or being creative or inventive, which is not the best definition in the context of the paragraph.

(e) freedom

This is an incorrect answer as democracy is in part about freedom and therefore this is not the closest meaning of latitude in this context.

16 Which of the following provides the best **definition** of the word 'democracy' as used in the passage?

(a) A popular government

(b) A political philosophy

(c) A republic

(d) A political belief

(e) A commonwealth

Question 16: *answer and rationale*

The question is asking you which statement provides the best **definition** of the word 'democracy', that is the meaning of the term in the context in which it is being used in the passage. In order to answer this question you will need to examine the passage very carefully. The highlighted statement and rationale is correct:

(a) A popular government

This is an incorrect answer as even though a 'democracy' could be described as 'a popular government' it is not the most appropriate definition in the context of the passage.

(b) A political philosophy

This is the correct answer as the passage describes democracy in terms of the theories of various philosophers including classical, contemporary and modern and is therefore more concerned with the study of democracy as a concept.

(c) A republic

This is an incorrect answer as even though a 'democracy' could be described as 'a republic' it is not the most appropriate definition in the context of the passage.

(d) A political belief

This is an incorrect answer as 'a political belief' implies a leaning to a single political theory rather than the fact of democracy being a wider concept.

(e) A commonwealth

This is an incorrect answer as even though a 'democracy' could be described as 'a commonwealth' it is not the most appropriate definition in the context of the passage.

17 What is the **main** argument made by Friedrich Hayek in relation to democracy?

(a) What is private should remain so

(b) People should resist state intervention

(c) Freedom comes at a price

(d) Freedom is of the highest value

(e) Privacy is of the highest value

Question 17: *answer and rationale*

The question is asking you to identify which one of the statements is the **main** argument of the passage. It does not suggest that a number of arguments will not be present. This is an evaluation as to whether the options provided are the main argument or not, in other words, whether they are true or false in relation to the question. In order to address this question it is necessary to read the passage thoroughly in order to follow the ideas and the structure of the issues to reach a conclusion as to which option is the main argument of the passage. The passage may contain several arguments that are relevant to the purpose of the passage as they help to build up a body of evidence. Therefore, it is important to examine the structure of the evidence as this may indicate what the main argument is. The highlighted statement and rationale is correct:

(a) What is private should remain so

This is an incorrect answer. It states in the passage 'Friedrich Hayek thinks democratic citizens should most value their freedom and use their democratic resources to resist intervention by the state in what should be private.' Retaining or obtaining 'privacy' is therefore part of the democratic model. It is not the main argument.

(b) People should resist state intervention

This is an incorrect answer as according to Friedrich Hayek freedom allows people to resist state intervention in what should be private therefore it is not the main argument.

(c) Freedom comes at a price

This is an incorrect answer as there is no mention in the passage of the price of freedom other than the quote 'democratic citizens should most value their freedom' which is not the same thing.

(d) Freedom is of the highest value

This is the correct answer as stated in the third paragraph: 'Friedrich Hayek thinks democratic citizens should most value their freedom.' This is therefore his main argument in relation to democracy.

(e) Privacy is of the highest value

This statement is an incorrect answer as even though Friedrich Hayek thinks privacy is important it is not his main argument.

18 What comes closest to Socrates' **meaning** of the phrase 'interests need to be banished from politics'?

(a) Without attachments and personal wealth

(b) Without spouses and children

(c) Without a spouse, children and private property

(d) Without wealth and private property

(e) Without family and private property

Question 18: *answer and rationale*

The question is asking you to identify the statement that has a similar **meaning** to the phrase 'interests need to be banished from politics'. The answer will require you to establish the context in which this phrase is used within the passage. It may be that more than one statement has some relationship to the answer and you need to determine the one that comes closet to or best describes the phrase 'interests need to be banished from politics'. The highlighted statement and rationale is correct:

(a) Without attachments and personal wealth

This is an incorrect answer as attachments and personal wealth are not specific enough. Attachments could be other family members even though personal wealth could be interpreted as property.

(b) Without spouses and children

This is an incorrect answer as Socrates also views the ownership of private property as a distraction.

(c) Without a spouse, children and private property

This is the correct answer as Socrates refers to spouses, children and the ownership of private property as being the 'interests' or attachments that distract leaders from having a reasoned approach to politics.

(d) Without wealth and private property

This is an incorrect answer as it does not include spouses and children whom Socrates also viewed as distractions.

(e) Without family and private property

This is an incorrect answer as Socrates was specifically referring to spouses and children and not family in general.

Passage 6: Animals and morality

These questions are related to the passage on page 47.

19 Which one of the following pair of traits is **not** descriptive of indirect theories?

(a) decision-making and autonomy

(b) rationality and discretion

(c) intrinsic value and consciousness

(d) inherent value and dependence

(e) mechanistic and willing

Question 19: *answer and rationale*

The question is asking you to identify the statement that contains the pair of traits that are not being used in the passage to describe 'indirect theories'. This seems reasonably straightforward and should be achieved by a process of elimination, i.e. determining which one of the pair of words has not been used to describe indirect theories. In order to answer this question you will need to examine the passage very carefully. The highlighted statement and rationale is correct.

(a) decision-making and autonomy

This is an incorrect answer as both are contained in the passage in support of the indirect theorists. 'Decision-making' is referred to as 'choice' in paragraph four, i.e. ' … only human beings are capable of standing back from their desires and choosing which course of action to take.' The reference to 'autonomy' can be found in the second sentence of paragraph two, i.e. ' … due to a lack of … autonomy.'

(b) rationality and discretion

This is an incorrect answer as both are contained in the passage in support of indirect theorists. Rationality is synonymous with reason contained in the second sentence of paragraph two i.e. ' … two, due to a lack of … reason … ' and 'humans' rationality' is also referred to in the second sentence of paragraph four i.e. ' ... willed by all rational individuals ... ' and the first sentence of paragraph six. 'Discretion' also means to be discerning or have choice, both of which apply to the thinking of the indirect theorists.

(c) intrinsic value and consciousness

This pair is an incorrect answer as both are contained in the passage in support of indirect theorists. Intrinsic value is referred to in paragraph four, final sentence, i.e. ' ... they therefore do not have any intrinsic value'. The reference to 'consciousness' can be found in the second sentence of paragraph two, i.e. ' ... due to a lack of consciousness ... ' and the first sentence in paragraph five, i.e. 'denials of animal consciousness ... '

(d) inherent value and dependence

This is the correct answer. Paragraph six states: 'Tom Regan argues for animal rights by relying on the concept of inherent value ... any being that is a subject-of-a-life is a being that has inherent value'. Interdependence relates to the concept that animals are not autonomous in the sense of human beings and rely on mutual support to survive.

(e) mechanistic and willing

This is an incorrect answer as both are contained in the passage in support of indirect theorists. Mechanistic is referred to in the first sentence of paragraph five, i.e. 'purely mechanistic terms'. The reference to 'willing' can be found in the third sentence in paragraph four, i.e. ' ... reliance on the notion of *willing*'.

20 Which one of the following statements comes **closest** to the criticism of indirect theories argued by Peter Singer?

(a) All life that can direct its own actions has inherent value irrespective of race or gender

(b) Indirect theories could be interpreted in a way that may expose human beings to discriminatory practices

(c) Humans' rationality, autonomy and ability to act morally cannot alone determine moral status

(d) The ability to choose a course of action should not determine the moral status of humans over animals

(e) There is no justification in denying animals moral status based on their lack of consciousness, reason, or autonomy

Question 20: *answer and rationale*

The question is asking you to identify which one of the statements comes **closest** to Peter Singer's criticism of indirect theories. It may be that more than one of the statements has some relationship to the answer and you need to determine the one that comes closest to or best describes the question asked. The highlighted statement and rationale is correct:

(a) **All life that can direct its own actions has inherent value irrespective of race or gender**

This is an incorrect answer as it combines three particular parts of the passage that do not reflect Singer's argument. The first part of the answer, 'life that can direct its own actions', is loosely taken from the beliefs of St Thomas Aquinas in paragraph three. 'Inherent value' is taken from the arguments of Tom Regan in the final paragraph. 'Irrespective of race or gender' is transposed from Singer's reference to 'racism and sexism' in paragraph six.

(b) **Indirect theories could be interpreted in a way that may expose human beings to discriminatory practices**

This is the correct answer. It come closest to the argument postulated by Singer in paragraph six i.e. ' … if we were to rely on a humans rationality, autonomy and the ability to act morally, as the basis of determining moral status, then we would justify a kind of discrimination against certain human beings that is structurally analogous to such practices as racism and sexism.'

(c) **Humans' rationality, autonomy and ability to act morally cannot alone determine moral status**

This is an incorrect answer as although it is taken from the wording of Singer's argument its context is compromised by a failure to include the full details of his argument.

(d) **The ability to choose a course of action should not determine the moral status of humans over animals**

This is an incorrect answer as it does not have any bearing on Singer's argument and has been constructed from other theorists within the passage.

(e) **There is no justification in denying animals moral status based on their lack of consciousness, reason, or autonomy**

This is an incorrect answer as it has no bearing on Singer's argument and has been extracted from paragraph two of the passage, i.e. '[Indirect theories] deny animals' moral status or equal consideration with humans due to a lack of consciousness, reason, or autonomy.'

21 In relation to the passage, which one of the following statements **best describes** Occam's Razor?

(a) A principle that suggests we should tend towards simpler theories

(b) Science tends to prefer a more logical explanation

(c) The simplest hypothesis proposed as an explanation of phenomena is more likely to be the true one

(d) Selecting the competing hypothesis that makes the fewest new assumptions

(e) The world is actually simple and simple accounts are more likely than complex ones to be true

Question 21: *answer and rationale*

The question is asking you to identify the one statement that **best describes** the meaning of 'Occam's Razor'. Quite clearly that part of the passage that deals directly with 'Occam's Razor' would be a first port of call to obtain a description. Such description could then be matched with the statements to identify the correct answer. Care must be taken where more than one statement is similar to identify the one that provides the best description of 'Occam's Razor'. The highlighted statement and rationale is correct.

(a) A principle that suggests we should tend towards simpler theories

This is the correct answer. In paragraph 5 it states 'Relying on the principle of parsimony in scientific explanation (commonly referred to as Occam's Razor) Descartes preferred to explain animal behaviour by relying on the simplest possible explanation of their behaviour. Since it is possible to explain animal behaviour without reference to inner episodes of awareness, doing so is simpler than relying on the assumption that animals are conscious, and is therefore the preferred explanation.'

(b) Science tends to prefer a more logical explanation

This is an incorrect answer as it is suggesting that science prefers a more 'logical' explanation as opposed to that which is contained in the passage, i.e. ' ... the simplest possible explanation ... '

(c) The simplest hypothesis proposed as an explanation of phenomena is more likely to be the true one

This is an incorrect answer as although Occam is Razor tends towards the 'simplest hypothesis', whether or not it 'is more likely to be the true one' is disputable and cannot be assumed from the contents of the passage.

(d) Selecting the competing hypothesis that makes the fewest new assumptions

This is an incorrect answer as it refers to the 'fewest new assumptions' as opposed to the 'simplest'.

(e) The world is actually simple and simple accounts are more likely than complex ones to be true

This is an incorrect answer. Although the principle of Occam's Razor provides for 'simple accounts', as with answer (c) above, whether they are more likely to be true than 'complex accounts' cannot be assumed from the contents of the passage.

Passage 7: immigration cap

These questions are related to the passage on page 49.

22 What is the **main** reason for the increase in net migration to Britain?

  (a) The fall in new national insurance registrations by Poles and other Eastern Europeans

  (b) Tier 1 non-EU people looking for work or self-employment

  (c) A surge in students from overseas coming to the UK to study

  (d) Tier 2 non-EU people who already had job offers

  (e) Fewer Britons leaving the UK to live abroad

Question 22: answer and rationale

The question is asking you to identify which one of the statements is the **main** reason for the increase in net migration to Britain. It does not suggest that a number of reasons will not be present. This is an evaluation as to whether the options provided are the main reason or not, in other words, whether they are true or false in relation to the question. In order to address this question it is necessary to read the passage thoroughly in order to follow the ideas and the structure of the argument to reach a conclusion as to which option is the main reason in relation to the question asked. The highlighted statement and rationale is correct:

(a) The fall in new national insurance registrations by Poles and other eastern Europeans

This is an incorrect answer. The passage states 'There was a fall of 14% in the past 12 months which included a 30% fall in new national insurance registrations by Poles and other eastern Europeans'. However, a fall in NI registrations cannot, clearly, be the main reason for increase in net migration.

(b) Tier 1 non-EU people looking for work or self-employment

This is an incorrect answer as the passage states that Tier 1 non-EU people 'will be cut from the present 13,000 per annum to 1,000.' Note must be taken of the fact that if the figure for people migrating from the UK is taken into account the number of people coming to the UK to work in the past 12 months has decreased. This is not the main reason for the increase in net migration to Britain.

(c) A surge in students from overseas coming to the UK to study

This is an incorrect answer. The passage states that 'there was a 3.7% rise in the number of overseas students coming to Britain. The total number of overseas students was 330,000 …' Five per cent of the 330,000 would be 16,500 extra students. This is not the main reason for the increase in net migration to Britain.

(d) Tier 2 non-EU people who already had job offers

This is an incorrect answer. The passage states that Tier 2 non-EU people 'will be cut by a fifth, from 28,000 a year down to 21,700'. There is no information as to whether the 28,000 was an increase or decrease on the previous 12 months. Also, as with answer (b) above, note must be taken of the fact that if the figure for people migrating from the UK is taken into account the number of people coming to the UK to work in the past 12 months has decreased.

(e) Fewer Britons leaving the UK to live abroad

This is the correct answer. The passage clearly states '… this rise was fuelled mostly by 60% fewer Britons leaving the country to live abroad – down from 90,000 to 36,000'. This is a difference of 54,000 and is the main reason for the increase in net migration to Britain.

23 All of the below illustrate migration trends in the UK **except**:

(a) The number of students from the Indian subcontinent using higher education is increasing

(b) Non-EU workers especially those from Eastern European countries are decreasing

(c) An increase in the number of people deciding against leaving the UK to live abroad

(d) An increase in the number of highly skilled workers migrating to the UK under the ICT system

(e) The number of non-EU highly skilled people who have job offers will be reduced

Question 23: *answer and rationale*

The question requires you to identify which of the statements does **not** correctly reflect an immigration trend as mentioned in the passage i.e. which of the statements is false. The highlighted statement and rationale is correct.

(a) The number of students from the Indian sub continent using higher education is increasing

This is incorrect as the answer is true. The passage states 'a surge in students coming to the UK from India – up by more than 15%.'

(b) Non-EU workers especially those from Eastern European countries are decreasing

This is incorrect as the answer is true. The passage states '…the actual number of people coming to work in Britain has continued to decline. There was a fall of 14% in the past 12 months'…'

(c) An increase in the number of people deciding against leaving the UK to live abroad

This is incorrect as the answer is true. The passage states '60% fewer Britons leaving the country to live abroad – down from 90,000 to 36,000.'

(d) An increase in the number of highly skilled workers migrating to the UK under the ICT system

This is correct as the answer is false. The passages states 'big global companies being allowed to continue to bring in non-EU workers under what is known as the Intra-Company Transfer (ICT) system.' It then goes on to state 'The ICT system will enable 22,500 non-EU workers to transfer each year…' It is a continuation of the ICT system and although the figure of 22,500 is given there is no comparative figure on which to determine whether this is an increase or decrease.

(e) The number of non-EU highly skilled people who have job offers will be reduced

This is incorrect as the answer is true. The passage states 'highly skilled people who already have job offers – this will be cut by a fifth, from 28,000 a year down to 21,700.'

24 Which one of the following statements **best describes** what is being suggested by the last paragraph of the passage?

(a) Immigrants are being allowed into the UK for the purposes of education outside the higher education sector without sufficient vigilance of any abuses

(b) Foreign nationals are being allowed entry to the UK for the purposes of family reunions or other family matters that may need to be better policed

(c) Migration to the UK whether within employment controls or not, might be subject to abuse by people seeking permanent residence and citizenship

(d) Another route into the UK may include illegal entry to the UK and further measures need to be considered in tackling this issue

(e) There is a hidden population of immigrants settling in the UK and controls need to counteract this problem

Question 24: *answer and rationale*

The question is asking you to identify the one statement that **best describes**, or the underlying message, contained in the last paragraph of the passage. Care must be taken where more than one statement is similar to identify the one that provides the best description of what is being suggested in the last passage. The highlighted statement and rationale is correct.

(a) Immigrants are being allowed into the UK for the purposes of education outside the higher education sector without sufficient vigilance of any abuses

This is an incorrect answer. Although the paragraph states: '… people come into the country, maybe for education…' it does not elaborate on this and in what form the 'system' is being abused. 'Education' is mentioned as one of three particular reasons why people come into the country so cannot be construed as an 'underlying message'.

(b) Foreign nationals are being allowed entry to the UK for the purposes of family reunions or other family matters that may need to be better policed

This is an incorrect answer. The paragraph states: '… people come into the country, maybe … for family reunion reasons …' As with education, 'family reunions' is mentioned as one of three particular reasons why people come into the country so cannot be construed as an 'underlying message'.

(c) Migration to the UK outside of employment controls may be subject to abuse by people seeking permanent residence and citizenship

This is the correct answer. The paragraph states that there is '… a need to look at the other routes by which people come into the country …', i.e. outside of 'employment controls'. It then goes on to state that '… hidden in these figures are two very big increases: one, of the number of students coming in, and the other, of the numbers of people settling here and gaining citizenship here.' Although it is not clear whether some of the people settling/gaining citizenship in the UK includes students, the issue of people settling/gaining citizenship is the underlying message of the paragraph and particularly so in contrast to the other statements offered.

(d) Another route into the UK may include illegal entry to the UK and further measures need to be considered in tackling this issue

This is an incorrect answer. Although this statement may in reality be true, 'illegal entry' is not alluded to in the paragraph and would definitely be a 'leap of faith' to be seriously considered.

(e) There is a hidden population of immigrants settling in the UK and controls need to counteract this problem

This is an incorrect answer. The paragraph refers to the increase in the number of students and people settling/gaining citizenship being ... hidden in these figures ...' but there is nothing to suggest a hidden population of immigrants settling in the UK.

Passage 8: origins of the universe

These questions are related to the passage on page 51.

25 Which one of the following statements is **not** part of Eriugena's definition of the universe?

(a) That which creates and is not created

(b) That which is created and creates

(c) That which is created and does not create

(d) That which neither is created nor creates

(e) That which creates the creation

Question 25: answer and rationale

The question requires you to determine which one of the five options does **not** form part of Eriugena's definition of the universe. You will need to consider this carefully and probably arrive at the answer by a process of elimination i.e. eliminating one statement at a time until you arrive at the correct answer. The highlighted statement and rationale is correct.

(a) That which creates and is not created

This is an incorrect answer as this option is contained within the passage, which refers to 'everything that exists', i.e. 'that which creates' and 'everything that does not exist', i.e. 'that which ... is not created'.

(b) That which is created and creates

This is an incorrect answer as this option is contained within the passage which states 'everything that ... has existed' i.e. 'that which is created' and 'everything that ... will exist' i.e. 'that which ... creates'.

(c) That which is created and does not create

This is an incorrect answer as this option is contained within the passage, which refers to 'everything that ... has existed', i.e. 'that which is created' and 'everything that ... will never exist', i.e. 'that which ... does not create'.

(d) That which neither is created nor creates

This is an incorrect answer as this option is contained within the passage which refers to 'everything that does not exist, has never existed and will never exist', i.e. 'that which neither is created nor creates'.

(e) That which creates the creation

This is the correct answer as the nature of the definition provides four distinct classes: that which creates and is not created; that which is created and creates; that which is created and does not create; that which neither is created nor creates. It does not include 'that which creates the creation'.

26 What comes closest to the **main** argument in the paragraph that begins **'Historically, many models of the cosmos and its origin ...'**?

(a) Abrahamic faiths do not believe in Einstein's theory

(b) Cosmology is the study of the origins of humanity

(c) Einstein proved the physical origin and evolution of the universe

(d) Theories of physical laws seek to explain the origins of the universe

(e) Astronomy has advanced the theory of creation over evolution

Question 26: answer and rationale

The question is asking you to identify the one statement that comes **closest** i.e. has a similar **meaning** to the main argument in the paragraph that begins *'Historically, many models of the cosmos and its origin'*. It may be that more than one statement has some relationship to the answer and you need to determine the one that comes closest to or best describes the question posed. The highlighted statement and rationale is correct:

(a) Abrahamic faiths do not believe in Einstein's theory

This is an incorrect answer. Although it might be assumed that those of Abrahamic faiths solely believe in the 'creation story' and a 'Creator-figure', this is not specifically dealt with in the passage and it may well be that some 'creationist believers' do accept Einstein's theories of origin and evolution.

(b) Cosmology is the study of the origins of humanity

This is an incorrect answer as the fact of cosmology being a study of the origins of humanity cannot be determined from the passage. In fact 'cosmology' has a wider meaning and can be defined as the study of the universe and, by extension, humanity's place within it.

(c) Einstein proved the physical origin and evolution of the universe

This is an incorrect answer and Einstein's 'General Theory of Relativity' is just that, a theory, i.e. an explanation of reality that has been thoroughly tested so that **most** scientists agree on it – not all scientists and certainly not all of humanity.

(d) Theories of physical laws seek to explain the origins of the universe

This is the correct answer as the passage states: 'Theories of an impersonal universe governed by physical laws were first proposed by the Greeks and Indians.' The passage then discusses Einstein's theory and later in the paragraph adds that ' ... theories of cosmology are based on general relativity ... '

(e) Astronomy has advanced the theory of creation over evolution

This is an incorrect answer; astronomy has probably advanced the theory of evolution more than that of creation, even though this cannot be determined from the passage. Astronomy, as well as being the study of celestial objects, is also concerned with evolution and the formation and development of the universe – in no sense is it a study supporting creationism.

27 Which of the following statements is true? Abrahamic religions:

(a) are the main religions in all countries across the world

(b) believe in the existence of one creator

(c) feature the same figures, histories and places

(d) do not believe in evolution

(e) are practised by over 50 per cent of the world's population

Question 27: answer and rationale

The question is asking you to identify which one of the statements is true about Abrahamic religions according to the information contained in the passage. The highlighted statement and rationale is correct.

(a) are the main religions in all countries across the world

This is an incorrect answer as although the passage states ' ... that 54% of the world's population consider themselves adherents of the Abrahamic religions', it does not state that this is the main religion 'in all countries of the world', i.e. some countries may have a lesser percentage of these religions.

(b) believe in the existence of one creator

This is the correct answer. The passage states ' ... all three are monotheistic (belief in the existence of one god) and conceive God to be a transcendent Creator-figure ... '

(c) feature the same figures, histories and places

This is an incorrect answer as the passage states that Arabic religions '… feature *many* of the same figures, histories and places …', i.e. they do not feature all the 'same figures, histories and places'.

(d) do not believe in evolution

This is an incorrect answer, as although the passage states that these religions believe in ' … a transcendent Creator-figure …' it does not state that such believers do not believe in evolution.

(e) are practised by over 50 per cent of the world's population

This is an incorrect answer as the passage states: 'It is estimated that 54% of the world's population consider themselves *adherents* of the Abrahamic religions … ' Being an 'adherent' of a religion is not the same as being a practising adherent.

28 In paragraph four of the passage what does the writer **mean** by the word 'transcendent'?

(a) outrageous

(b) supernatural

(c) nonsensical

(d) magnificent

(e) bizarre

Question 28: *answer and rationale*

The question is asking you to identify a word with a **meaning** that is the same, or very similar to, another word, in this case the word 'transcendent'. Put simply you are looking for a synonym of 'transcendent'. The answer will require you to establish the context in which the word 'transcendent' is used within the fourth paragraph of the passage. It may be that more than one word has some relationship to the answer and you need to determine the one that comes closest to or best describes the word 'transcendent'. The highlighted statement and rationale is correct:

(a) outrageous

This is an incorrect answer as 'outrageous' is an antonym of 'transcendent' and basically means going beyond all standards of what is right and descent. An antonym is a word which has the opposite meaning to another, although not necessarily in all its senses.

(b) supernatural

This is an incorrect answer as 'supernatural' means anything above or beyond what one holds to be natural or exists outside natural law and the observable universe. It is not an antonym or synonym of 'transcendent'.

(c) nonsensical

This is an incorrect answer as 'nonsensical' is an antonym of 'transcendent' and basically means something absurd, foolish or irrational.

(d) magnificent

This is the correct answer in the context of the passage as 'magnificent' means something that is glorious, marvellous, superb, wonderful, beyond or above the range of normal or physical human experience'. 'Magnificent is a synonym of 'transcendent'.

(e) bizarre

This is an incorrect answer as 'bizarre' is an antonym of 'transcendent' and basically means something unusual, peculiar or out of the ordinary.

Passage 9: early years education

These questions are related to the passage on page 53.

29 Which of the following phrases **best describes** the Reggio Emilia approach to education?

(a) Child-centred approach to learning

(b) Philosophy of 'seeing oneself' and of constructing one's identity

(c) Expressing skills through a 'hundred languages'

(d) Powerful experience of adults and children collaborating

(e) An open environment in which learning can flourish naturally

Question 29: answer and rationale

The question is asking you to identify the one statement that **best describes** the Reggio Emilia's approach to education. Care must be taken where more than one statement is similar to identify the one that provides the best description of what is being suggested in the last passage. The highlighted statement and rationale is correct.

(a) Child-centred approach to learning

This is the correct answer. The whole tenet of the passage is about early years children in Reggio Emilia schools having considerable involvement in and influence over their own learning. It specifically states: 'Loris Malaguzzi, founder of the project, valued highly the benefits of a child-centred approach to learning.'

(b) Philosophy of 'seeing oneself' and of constructing one's identity

This is an incorrect answer. This is an integral part of the Reggio Emilia philosophy but does not best describe its overall approach to education.

(c) Expressing skills through a 'hundred languages'

This is an incorrect answer. Again it is an integral part of the approach used by Reggio Emilia schools but does not best describe its overall approach to education.

(d) Powerful experience of adults and children collaborating

This is an incorrect answer. Similarly, it is an important part of creating a child-centred approach to early years schooling but does not best describe its overall approach to education.

(e) An open environment in which learning can flourish naturally

This is an incorrect answer. It is an important part of Reggio Emilia philosophy but again does not best describe its overall approach to education.

30 The **most important** fact that the writer seeks to convince the reader of is:

(a) A wide variety of media, such as art, movement, language and music, is crucial to allow children to express themselves

(b) Real learning is achieved in an education system that encourages and fosters a creative learning environment

(c) The UK does not encourage a child-centred approach to early years education

(d) Children who learn kinaesthetically and visually are better developed in their early years of education

(e) The role of the environment is crucial as a motivating and animating force in the promotion of the myriad ways of learning

Question 30: *answer and rationale*

The question is asking you to identify which one of the statements is the **most important** fact that the writer seeks to convince the reader of. It does not suggest that a number of facts will not be present. This is an evaluation as to whether the options provided are the most important fact or not, in other words, whether they are true or false in relation to the question. In order to address this question it is necessary to read the passage thoroughly in order to follow the ideas and the structure of the argument to reach a conclusion as to which option is the most important fact of the passage. The passage may contain several facts that are relevant to the purpose of the passage as they help to build up a body of evidence. Therefore, it is important to examine the structure of the argument as this may indicate the most important fact. The highlighted statement and rationale is correct:

(a) **A wide variety of media, such as art, movement, language and music, is crucial to allow children to express themselves**

This is an incorrect answer. A wide variety of media such as art, etc. is stated in the passage but this is one of a number of facts identified by the writer and is not the best answer to the question posed.

(b) **Real learning is achieved in an education system that encourages and fosters a creative learning environment**

This is the correct answer. Creativity or creative learning is mentioned three times in the passage. Two of these extracts are '… creating an open environment of trust and wonder in which creativity is allowed to flourish naturally' and '… several features of the Reggio Emilia pre-schools which make them particularly conducive to creative learning.' However, the most important extract is at the end of the passage, i.e. 'A system that encouraged and fostered creativity beyond that of the written word would, at the very least, give all children more options. At its best, it could revolutionise our understanding of what real learning is about!'

(c) **The UK does not encourage a child-centred approach to early years education**

This is an incorrect answer. The passage does not specifically state that the UK does not encourage a child-centred approach. Although it does state that the UK system favours those who learn best through language and text over those who learn kinaesthetically and visually, this alone does not mean a child-centred approach is not in use.

(d) **Children who learn kinaesthetically and visually are better developed in their early years of education**

This is an incorrect answer. There is no evidence in the passage to substantiate this statement. No information is provided as to the achievements of the children in the Reggio Emilia schools compared with children in the UK.

(e) **The role of the environment is crucial as a motivating and animating force in the promotion of the myriad ways of learning**

This is an incorrect answer. The role of the environment is specifically stated in the passage but this is one of a number of facts identified by the writer and is not the best answer to the question posed.

31 Which one of the following statements could be substituted in place of Abbott and Nutbrown's observation '**The tetrahedron with the mirrored interior is often to be found there ...** ' and still retain the same meaning?

(a) A triangular pyramid with a mirrored interior is often found in the piazza

(b) A light and spacious building with a mirrored interior is often found there

(c) A cylindrical structure with a mirrored interior is often found in the piazza

(d) A terraced construction with a mirrored interior is often found there

(e) An angular structure with a mirrored interior is often found in the piazza

Question 31: *answer and rationale*

The question is asking you to determine which one of the alternative statements would replace existing text and retain the same meaning or context. Be aware that more than one of the options may be quite similar and you need to make a judgment as to which one is the correct answer. The highlighted statement and rationale is correct.

(a) A triangular pyramid with a mirrored interior is often found in the piazza

This is the correct answer. A *tetrahedron* is a triangular pyramid and in relation to the piazza the passage states: '"Distinctive in all the … preschools is the piazza: the central meeting place where children from all around the school share their play and conversations together. The tetrahedron with the mirrored interior is often to be found there …"'

(b) A light and spacious building with a mirrored interior is often found there

This is an incorrect answer. Although the *tetrahedron* may be 'a light and spacious building' this is not the preferred answer.

(c) A cylindrical structure with a mirrored interior is often found in the piazza

This is an incorrect answer. A *tetrahedron* is a triangular pyramid and not a cylindrical structure.

(d) A terraced construction with a mirrored interior is often found there

This is an incorrect answer. A *tetrahedron* is a triangular pyramid and not a terraced construction.

(e) An angular structure with a mirrored interior is often found in the piazza

This is an incorrect answer. A *tetrahedron* is a triangular pyramid and not an angular structure.

32 In relation to the passage, which one of the following statements about early years education is correct?

(a) In the UK adults have little confidence in their early years children's ability to succeed

(b) Reggio Emilia early years children are far more developed in constructing their own identity than children in the UK

(c) In the UK there is minimal support for early years children who learn by actually carrying out a physical activity

(d) Reggio Emilia children have a better relationship with adults than children in the UK

(e) In the UK early years children do not have qualified artists who are members of staff

Question 32: *answer and rationale*

The question requires you to consider each of the five statements to determine which one is evidenced by the information presented in the passage. This will require careful reading of the passage to eliminate statements or otherwise. The highlighted statement and rationale is correct.

(a) In the UK adults have little confidence in their early years children's ability to succeed

This is an incorrect answer. The passage states that in the Reggio Emilia approach '... adults also had unfailing confidence in the children's ability to succeed.' This subject area commences 'By contrast by what we might find in many UK settings ...' Therefore the unequivocal answer statement is incorrect.

(b) Reggio Emilia early years children are far more developed in constructing their own identity than children in the UK

This is an incorrect answer. The passage states the Reggio Emilia approach has a '... central philosophy of "seeing oneself" and of constructing one's identity'. However, there is no mention or contrast with the development of identity for UK children. Further information would be needed for this answer to be correct.

(c) In the UK there is minimal support for early years children who learn by actually carrying out a physical activity

This is the correct answer as the passage clearly states '... the UK works against those who learn kinaesthetically and visually'. Kinaesthetic learning is a learning style in which learning takes place by the child actually carrying out a physical activity.

(d) **Reggio Emilia children have a better relationship with adults than children in the UK**

This is an incorrect answer. In relation to Reggio Emilia the passage states that '… adults and children learn that collaboration is a powerful experience … ' and '… adults also had unfailing confidence in the children's ability to succeed.' There is no information on adult–child relations in the UK and more information would be required to determine the validity of the statement.

(e) **In the UK early years children do not have qualified artists who are members of staff**

This is an incorrect answer. In relation to the Reggio Emilia approach the passage states: 'Another distinctive feature … is the atelier, the art studio, where children work with the atelerista … the qualified artist who is a member of staff.' Again, there is no comparative information about the UK as to whether qualified artists are employed as members of staff.

Passage 10: the aging process

These questions are related to the passage on page 55.

33 Which one of the following statements does **not** introduce a new argument?

(a) The condition of the blood is at the core of the immune system

(b) What a person eats can damage their physiology

(c) Changes in hormones control aging

(d) Positive thinking can extend human life

(e) Genetics may determine the length of human life

Question 33: answer and rationale

The question is asking you to identify the statement that is already evidenced in the passage i.e. it does **not** introduce a new argument. The four incorrect statements will be introducing new material so you will need to know the content and context of the passage in order to eliminate these arguments. The highlighted statement and rationale is correct.

(a) **The condition of the blood is at the core of the immune system**

This is an incorrect answer, as 'blood' has not been specifically mentioned in any of the theories referred to in the passage.

(b) What a person eats can damage their physiology

This is the correct answer as it is referred to in the passage under the 'wear and tear' theory that states: '... the body accumulates damage from interior ... factors, such as poor diet.'

(c) Changes in hormones control aging

This is an incorrect answer. 'Changes in hormones' is not referred to within the passage and is therefore introducing a new argument.

(d) Positive thinking can extend human life

This is an incorrect answer. 'Positive thinking' is not referred to within the passage and is therefore introducing a new argument.

(e) Genetics may determine the length of human life

This is an incorrect answer as 'genetics' is not referred to within the passage and is therefore introducing a new argument.

34 Which, if any, of the three theories would account for psychological degeneration during the aging process?

(a) None of the theories

(b) Wear and tear theory

(c) Cellular theory

(d) Immunity theory

(e) All of the theories

Question 34: answer and rationale

The question is asking you to determine if the question posed can be accounted for by the description in the passage of one or more of the three theories. You need to establish if 'psychological degeneration during the aging process' is contained in any of the theories by carefully reading the passage. The highlighted statement and rationale is correct.

(a) None of the theories

This is an incorrect answer as psychological deterioration of the human body during the aging process can be accounted for by the theories.

(b) Wear and tear theory

This is an incorrect answer as 'wear and tear' proposes that as machines wear out, each human's physiology is affected in a similar way. This physiological affect applies to the deterioration of the body's organs and this could include the brain leading to psychological degeneration. However, this is not the correct answer as the other two theories can also account for this degeneration.

(c) Cellular theory

This is an incorrect answer as cellular theory deals with errors in cell division contributing to the degenerative conditions experienced in old age. The diseases arising from these errors could include the brain and lead to psychological degeneration. However, this is not the correct answer as the other two theories can also account for this degeneration.

(d) Immunity theory

This is an incorrect answer as immunity theory deals with the immune system in the body becoming less efficient providing for an increase in harmful cells that can cause damage to the body leading to degeneration. Obviously the brain being part of the body can be equally affected thus being susceptible to psychological degeneration. However, this is not the correct answer as the other two theories can also account for this degeneration.

(e) All of the theories

This is the correct answer as all three theories, as described in (b), (c) and (d) above, can account for psychological degeneration in old age.

35 What do 'cellular theory' and 'immunity theory' have in common?

(a) Associated with errors in cell division

(b) Explain the theories of aging at a physiological level

(c) Account for the changes within the human body as people age

(d) Antibodies are unable to destroy toxic cells

(e) Cell impairment works in a self-destructive way

Question 35: answer and rationale

The question is asking you to identify which statement contains information that is common to both the 'cellular theory' and the 'immunity theory'. By asking this question it is obvious that these two theories only have one thing in common. The highlighted statement and rationale is correct.

(a) Associated with errors in cell division

This is an incorrect answer. In the explanation of 'cellular theory' the passage states "…the theory is concerned with the ways in which errors in cell division occurring throughout life...' The 'immunity theory' is concerned with harmful cells that cannot be 'killed off' by the immune system.

(b) Explain the theories of aging at a physiological level

This is an incorrect answer. In relation to 'immunity theory' the passage states that this 'is explained at a physiological rather than a cellular level'. The 'cellular theory' is explained at a cellular level.

(c) Account for the changes within the human body as people age

This is the correct answer. Both theories are trying to account for the changes that occur within the human body throughout life and particularly for the later years of old age.

(d) Antibodies are unable to destroy toxic cells

This is an incorrect answer. The cellular theory considers toxic substances and their effects on the body, while 'immunity theory' does not specifically refer to 'toxic cells' though these might relate to mutated cells. In any event this is not common to both theories.

(e) Cell impairment works in a self-destructive way

This is an incorrect answer. In relation to the variation of immunity theory, 'auto-immune theory', the passage states '... resulting in the auto-immune antibodies working in a self-destructive way'. There is no reference to this in the information on 'cellular theory'.

Passage 11: taxonomy of charities

These questions are related to the passage on page 57.

36 Which of the following does the writer present as **paradoxical?**

    (a) Some public schools have charity status

    (b) There has been a decline in charitable donations

    (c) Donors do not research the charity they give to

    (d) Charities should be ranked according to their benefit to society

    (e) People have given more money to a donkey sanctuary than to a welfare charity.

Question 36: *answer and rationale*

The question is asking you which one of the statements does the writer present as a **paradox**. A paradox is a seemingly true statement or group of statements that lead to a contradiction or a situation which seems to defy logic or intuition, and is also used for situations that are merely surprising. Therefore you are searching for the statement that might defy logic or be surprising. The highlighted statement and rationale is correct:

(a) Some public schools have charity status

This is an incorrect answer. The fact that some public schools have charity status may be illogical to some; however, the writer is not using this statement paradoxically.

(b) There has been a decline in charitable donations

This is an incorrect answer; it is just a statement of fact supported by statistical information.

(c) Donors do not research the charity they give to

This is an incorrect answer: although it may seem surprising, it is a statement of fact and not a paradox.

(d) Charities should be ranked according to their benefit to society

This is an incorrect answer. It is the suggestion being put forward for a 'taxonomy of charities' and is not being used paradoxically.

(e) People have given more money to a donkey sanctuary than to a welfare charity

This statement is the correct answer as the writer is presenting the fact that 'more money has been given to a donkey sanctuary than a charity for abuse and violence against women' as paradoxical.

37 Based on the passage, which of the following would be the **main** priority of classification for the 'taxonomy of charities'?

(a) Merit

(b) Good cause

(c) Personal preference

(d) Beneficiary donors

(e) Social good

Question 37: *answer and rationale*

The question is asking you, based on the passage, which of the following would be the **main** priority of classification for the 'taxonomy of charities'. Understanding the content and context of the passage is crucial to arrive at the correct answer. The highlighted statement and rationale is correct:

(a) Merit

This is the correct answer as 'merit' encompasses all the possible parameters for classifying the most and least worthwhile causes, which may include some of the other options.

(b) Good cause

This is an incorrect answer as what constitutes a good cause could be a matter of personal preference, which may be a least worthwhile cause. Therefore it would not be the main priority but that is not to say that it would not form part of the overall criteria.

(c) Personal preference

This is an incorrect answer as personal preference may be based on ill-informed giving. Nevertheless, as a large number of current donors use this criterion it may form part of the overall criteria.

(d) Beneficiary donors

This is an incorrect answer. Donors who feel they are repaying a benefit received are an important source of charitable donations but this would not be the main priority of classification.

(e) Social good

This is an incorrect answer even though the introductory paragraph suggests that charities should be ranked according to their benefit to society. However, this would only form part of the assessment of worthiness.

38 What is the voluntary sector's **main** objection to a 'taxonomy of charities'?

(a) People may donate to the bigger charities

(b) It may take away personal choice

(c) It may affect the decision-making of donors

(d) People may donate less to charities

(e) People may not donate to charities that have helped them

Question 38: *answer and rationale*

The question is asking you to identify which one of the statements describes the voluntary sector's **main** objection to a 'Taxonomy of Charities'. It does not suggest that other objections will not be present. This is an evaluation as to whether the options provided are the main objection or not, in other words, whether they are true or false in relation to the question. In order to address this question it is necessary to read the passage thoroughly in order to follow the ideas and the structure of the argument to reach a conclusion as to which option is the fundamental objection of the voluntary sector. The highlighted statement and rationale is correct:

(a) People may donate to the bigger charities

This is an incorrect answer as it is not stated or implied in the passage.

(b) It may take away personal choice

This is an incorrect answer, as any individual will always have the right to exercise their personal choice when making charitable donations. The view in the passage is that this personal choice may be affected.

(c) It may affect the decision-making of donors

This is the correct answer. As stated in the second paragraph, charity bosses and the leader of the Association of Chief Executives of Voluntary Organisations have concerns that the current personal preferences of donors would be affected and that this may impact on the decision as to which charity they would donate to.

(d) People may donate less to charities

This is an incorrect answer as it is not the main concern of the voluntary sector, albeit a concern generally. The concern is more related to the impact the 'taxonomy of charities' may have on the decision-making process of donors.

(e) People may not donate to charities that have helped them

This is an incorrect answer as it is not the main concern of the voluntary sector. The concern is more related to the impact the 'taxonomy of charities' may have on the decision-making process of donors.

39 Which of the following is **not stated** in the passage.

(a) The number of Britons donating to charities is less now than ten years ago.

(b) Social good is not the main priority of charitable donors.

(c) Public schools can have charitable status.

(d) The amount donated by Britons to charities was less last year than previous years.

(e) Almost a quarter of those that donate to charity have a personal reason for doing so.

Question 39: *answer and rationale*

The question is asking you to identify which statement is **inferred** but not directly stated by the writer but does follow logically from statements made in the passage. Again you are looking for which of the options is true or false (correct or incorrect) given the question. There are two types of statements that would be incorrect. The first type of potential answer would be one where the proposition is directly stated as the question asks you to identify issues, which are not directly stated. It follows that anything that is explicit (actually stated) must be incorrect in the light of the instruction you have been given in this particular question. The highlighted statement and rationale is correct:

(a) **The number of Britons donating to charities is less now than ten years ago**

This is an incorrect answer as it is clearly stated in the passage 'Ten years ago, 68% of the population gave to charities but the current figure has dropped to 54%.'

(b) **Social good is not the main priority of charitable donors**

This is an incorrect answer as it is stated in the penultimate paragraph that the lowest percentage (14%) of those studied gave for this reason therefore social good is not the main priority of charitable donors and it is **stated**.

(c) **Public schools can have charitable status**

This statement is an incorrect answer as it is stated in the third paragraph 'The fact that some public schools have charity status...'

(d) **The amount donated by Britons to charities was less last year than previous years**

This statement is the correct answer. The statistics quoted in paragraph four indicate a decline over the last ten years in the number of people who have donated to charities and quotes the amount donated last year. It **cannot be inferred** from these figures that the actual amount donated last year was less than previous years as those that did donate could have donated higher amounts.

(e) **Almost a quarter of those that donate to charity have a personal reason for doing so**

This statement is an incorrect answer as it is stated in the penultimate paragraph 'that 23% of donors support charities that have directly benefited them' therefore as 23% is almost a quarter this is a personal reason.

Passage 12: Critical reflection

These questions are related to the passage on page 59.

40 Which one of the following sentences serves **to develop** the information contained in paragraph five of the passage?

(a) Reflection allows for the critical analysis and evaluation of both positive and negative experiences

(b) Be aware that overly reflecting on negative experiences can cause anxiety and defensiveness

(c) In experiential learning, the learner changes from an active participant in an experience to a reflector

(d) The development of the self as a critical practitioner is essential

(e) In practice critical thinking and learning are essential when debating reflection

Question 40: *answer and rationale*

The question is asking you to identify the most appropriate sentence that serves **to develop** the information contained in the final paragraph of the passage. This requires you to obtain an understanding of the content and context of the final paragraph and look at which sentence makes the most sense of developing it, and obviously bears some relationship to the information contained in the sentence. If there is more than one sentence that would develop the paragraph you need to make a judgement as to which would be the 'best fit'.

(a) Reflection allows for the critical analysis and evaluation of both positive and negative experiences

This is an incorrect answer as this is already stated in the first paragraph of the passage it states 'critical reflection…to critically analyse and evaluate experiences…'

(b) Be aware that overly reflecting on negative experiences can cause anxiety and defensiveness

This is the correct answer. The first sentence of the paragraph states 'However, placing oneself at the centre of an event or experience can lead to a preoccupation with the self than can border on self-absorption.' The statement builds on this 'self-absorption' by identifying the downside of reflecting on negative experiences.

(c) In experiential learning, the learner changes from an active participant in an experience to a reflector

This is an incorrect answer. This statement refers 'reflector' as part of experiential learning and is not associated with the contents of the passage.

(d) The development of the self as a critical practitioner is essential

This is an incorrect answer. This is a general statement and could sit anywhere within the passage. If used it would probably be best placed at the beginning or end of the passage.

(e) In practice critical thinking and learning are essential when debating reflection

This is an incorrect answer. This may well be the case but does not develop the information in the paragraph under discussion.

41 Which one of these phrases **best** sums up the idea of 'critical reflection'?

(a) The processes of being consciously deliberative or analytical

(b) The ability to reflect, to be self-aware and to question

(c) The concept of self-awareness in evaluating skills and beliefs

(d) The processes involved in developing personal ability

(e) Being self-aware, analysing and evaluating practical experiences

Question 41: *answer and rationale*

The question is almost asking you to define the meaning of 'critical reflection' using the information provided in the passage. It may be that more than one of the statements sums up the idea of 'critical thinking' but you need to find the **best** statement by carefully reading the passage. The highlighted statement and rationale is correct.

(a) The processes of being consciously deliberative or analytical

This is an incorrect answer. 'Being consciously deliberative or analytical' although part of 'critical reflection' is not the most comprehensive and best way to sum up its meaning.

(b) The ability to reflect and to question

This is an incorrect answer. Although the ability to 'reflect and to question' are part of critical reflection, the statement has failed to include the important concept of 'self-awareness'.

(c) The concept of self-awareness in evaluating skills and beliefs

This is an incorrect answer. This statement is not comprehensive, e.g. it does not include 'analytical skills', and 'evaluating skills and beliefs' has failed to mention 'attitudes', etc.

(d) The development of the self as a critical practitioner is essential

This is an incorrect answer as this is a general statement of intent and does not provide any meaning of 'critical reflection'.

(e) Being self-aware, analysing and evaluating practical experiences

This is the correct answer. This is the best answer as it contains all the strands of 'critical reflection', i.e. self-awareness, analysis and evaluation of experiences.

42 In paragraph 3 of the passage which one of the following words does **not** mean consciously deliberative'?

(a) Intuitive

(b) Planned

(c) Premeditated

(d) Intentional

(e) Calculated

Question 42: *answer and rationale*

The question is asking you to define the meaning of 'consciously deliberative' in order to eliminate four of the five options provided to arrive at the correct answer. 'Consciously' means to be aware of, to be awake, or to know what we are doing. 'Deliberative' means intentionally or purposefully. The word that is sought is therefore something other than being aware of doing something intentionally. The highlighted statement and rationale is correct.

(a) Intuitive

This is the correct answer. 'Intuitive' means to be instinctive, spontaneous or innate. However, 'consciously' means intentionally or knowingly, and 'deliberative' has a similar meaning in that it describes something that describes done or marked by full consciousness of the nature or effects.

(b) Planned

This is an incorrect answer as 'planned' means intended, premeditated or deliberate and is therefore similar to 'consciously deliberative'.

(c) Premeditated

This is an incorrect answer as 'premeditated' means conscious, thought out or planned and is therefore similar to 'consciously deliberative'.

(d) Intentional

This is an incorrect answer as 'intentional' means premeditated, calculated or planned and is therefore similar to 'consciously deliberative'.

(e) Calculated

This is an incorrect answer as 'calculated' covers all the descriptions provided in answers (b) to (d) above.

It would be inappropriate not to have a chapter on essay writing where an essay forms part of the test. However, this chapter is not intended to be an in-depth or academic study of essay writing. Instead it contains practical advice that will assist any student preparing for Section B of the LNAT®.

The requirement is for candidates to produce a reasoned and substantiated argument justifying their response to a question chosen from a list of five questions provided. Palgrave; Crème, P and Lea, M (1997) *Writing at University: A Guide for Students*. Open University Press.

It cannot be stressed enough that the best preparation for essay writing (in addition to this chapter) is to read regularly one of the broadsheets and some well-written novels. All the texts available on essay writing emphasise that the more literature we read, the better our writing style. Reading improves our thought processes and extends the range of words at our disposal. You will have seen with the critical reasoning examples that some of the questions are based on articles from broadsheets and this really underpins their importance – particularly to the LNAT® examiners.

The purpose of this chapter is to:

- examine the LNAT® requirements and example questions
- provide a structured approach to essay writing
- develop writing techniques which are concerned with the use of 'critical' thought in essay writing
- develop the use of grammar, sentences and punctuation in essay writing.

11. LNAT® requirement and sample test

This section considers the requirements of Section B of the test and examines questions of a similar format to the LNAT®.

The requirement is for candidates to produce a reasoned and substantiated argument justifying their response to a question chosen from a list of five questions provided. The time allowed for this part of the test is 40 minutes. As with Part A, this is on-screen, with a window being provided for you to type in the text of your essay. There are 'cut', 'copy', 'paste', 'undo' and 'redo' functions but there is no 'spell check' or other word-processing functions. You are required to ideally write 500–600 words and at the most 750 – there is a built-in 'word count' at the bottom of the screen. Note that anything written beyond 750 words will not be read by the LNAT® university. The time remaining for the essay is displayed at the top of the screen. Below is an example for this part of the test:

Section B: essay

Answer one of the following questions.

1   What are the arguments for and against the introduction of proportional representation in general elections?

2   Is it the best policy for the UK government to be more concerned with sending young people to university than increasing the manufacturing skills base through work-based training programmes?

3   A-level results are now meaningless following the year on year increase in pass levels. Do you agree?

4   Is it true to say that the British Broadcasting Corporation is still perceived as reporting the news objectively throughout the world?

5   The international agreements on the emission of greenhouse gases are ineffective. How would you respond to this statement?

12. Structured approach

To ensure that an essay is relevant to the question being answered, is correctly structured, and has sufficient and consistent evidence and examples in support of your arguments, it is advisable to make use of a simple model which identifies a staged approach to essay writing.

It is important that each of the following stages is considered separately:

- Identify what is being asked in each of the questions
- Identify the question that you would be best able to answer
- Brainstorm the issues and arguments relevant to the question
- Plan the structure
- Write the essay
- Revision

You may be one of those people in the top few per cent of the population who can just write a well-reasoned essay without any preparation or planning. If you are not then time spent on the first four stages will be time well spent before you start actually writing the essay. Give yourself up to 10 MINUTES for these four stages, probably a couple of minutes each on the first two stages and five or six minutes on the next two stages. You can use the screen to time yourself as the time remaining will be shown in the top right-hand corner. Control your natural urge to skip these stages and properly plan and prepare – as the old saying goes, 'failing to plan is planning to fail'!

Identify what is being asked in each of the questions

Like the majority of the population, at the outset you may convince yourself that you know next to nothing about any of the essay questions on offer. DON'T PANIC! No matter what the subject there will be very few occasions where you are unable to come up with a number of relevant ideas to form a useful structure from your own knowledge and experience - and invariably this is the process that is of interest to the examiners.

In your anxiety you will want to get on with writing the essay but you should resist this temptation and spend a few minutes making sure you will be answering the question being asked. The question will usually provide you with both the structure of the essay and sometimes the abilities you are required to display.

It sounds obvious, but it is important to be absolutely sure what the question is asking you to do. It has often been the case that a person reads into the question something that isn't there and so writes the whole essay without answering the question.

Let's look at a couple of questions from the example essay topics given above and unpack them to determine what is being asked:

1. **What are the arguments for and against the introduction of proportional representation in general elections?**

This question can be broken down easily into four constituent parts, i.e. 'What are the arguments/for and against/the introduction of proportional representation/in general elections?'

*   'What are the arguments' is essentially asking for the reasons for and against the introduction of proportional representation ... Reasons include evidence, principles, assumptions and logical inferences or causal connections which are given to support judgements and recommendations. Further details about arguments, reasons and conclusions are provided on page 118 under the heading 'critical thinking'.

*   'for and against' is asking for the pros and cons of the introduction of proportional representation ... This is not asking you for your own ideas and thoughts on the issue and you need to keep focussed on what is being asked.

*   'the introduction of proportional representation/in general elections' are both very specific and your arguments must retain a focus on these.

2. **What is your response to the view that the international agreements on the emission of greenhouse gases are ineffective?**

This question can be broken down into five constituent parts, though the last two parts might preferably be combined, i.e. 'What is your response/to the view/that the international agreements/on the emission of greenhouse gases/are ineffective?

- 'What is your response' is asking for your reaction to the question posed. It invites you to present both evidence, principles, assumptions and logical inferences, as well as your own thoughts on the issue.
- 'to the view' is suggesting that there are apparently opposing views to the one given and they should be raised and considered in the essay.
- 'that the international agreements' is quite specific and in answering this question you would need to demonstrate a certain amount of knowledge in this area.
- 'on the emission of greenhouse gases' is quite specific and in answering the question you would need to demonstrate a certain amount of knowledge of the causes and impact of the emission of greenhouse gases.
- 'are ineffective' is making a definitive statement which should be considered in that light and contested or otherwise.

The two examples given above may appear somewhat long-winded. In reality this would not be the case. It would probably take less than a minute to identify and note down the constituent parts of any particular question to make sure your essay will directly answer the chosen question.

Identify the question that you would be best able to answer

There may be more than one question that you feel able to answer but you need to consider which one would allow you to best demonstrate your analytical abilities. The examiners are looking for a 'well-reasoned' essay.

Some questions may lend themselves to a more 'argumentative' approach, examining the various pros and cons of the issue(s) raised and forming some kind of conclusions, for example, 'What are the arguments for and against the introduction of proportional representation in general elections?'

Other questions may require a more analytical or critical approach requiring you to show you can identify more difficult abstract concepts, for example, 'What is your response to the view that the international agreements on the emission of greenhouse gases are ineffective?' Both types of question will obviously influence the way in which your essay is structured and some type of structure should already be forming in your mind, even subconsciously, before you move on to the next stage.

Brainstorm the issues and arguments relevant to the question

There is no doubt that when universities examine essays they are looking for good analytical ability in order to distinguish between better performers. It is suggested by some academic writers that analysis and brainstorming are two separate concepts. In analysis the individual identifies and analyses the concepts and implications of the question. They then write down their own ideas identifying one concept's essential characteristics. In the other concept the individual is simply brainstorming their own ideas. The analysis concept requires considerable time to unravel and consequently is not advised for use in essays under test conditions.

Brainstorming is coming up with a number of ideas from your own knowledge and experience and writing them down even if they are not relevant. You can easily discard the irrelevant ideas afterwards. Essentially, the product of brainstorming will provide the basis for the essay structure and the content.

There are a number of different techniques available when brainstorming: it can be totally organic and unstructured, or more structured methods such as mind mapping and the use of mnemonics. You may be familiar with a particular method and if so use it. Some people find mind mapping beneficial, others don't. If you haven't previously used this method and it appeals to you buy a book on it, there are plenty available. We will concentrate on the assistance to brainstorming that can be provided by mnemonics, solely in relation to writing essays.

Children are often taught to remember the colours of the rainbow using the mnemonic, 'Richard of York gave battle in vain' – red, orange, yellow, green, blue, indigo and violet. Students would normally use mnemonics where they are learnt for specific knowledge-based examinations.

There are two useful mnemonics that are often used for providing a structure into which you can place your ideas and thoughts or which themselves supply a vehicle and structure for encouraging such ideas and thoughts.

SWOT analysis

The first mnemonic, often useful in answering 'argue for and against' types of question (though also used for more open questions), is referred to as a **SWOT** analysis – **S**trengths, **W**eaknesses, **O**pportunities, **T**hreats.

We will use this mnemonic in examining the example essay question, 'What are the arguments for and against the introduction of proportional representation in general elections?'

Strengths

- May encourage people to vote
- More representative government

Weaknesses

- Hung parliaments
- Lack of leadership
- Weak government

Opportunities

- Focus on the needs of the electorate
- Policies represent the needs of the electorate
- Greater democracy
- More say in government
- Liberal Democrats' manifesto

Threats

- Policies become ineffective
- Government over-representative of minority groups
- All talk and no action

PESTEL *analysis*

The second mnemonic provides a broad 'analysis' of a question and is referred to as **PESTEL** analysis – **P**olitical, **E**conomic, **S**ocial, **T**echnical, **E**nvironmental, **L**egal.

We will use this mnemonic in examining the example essay question, 'What is your response to the view that the international agreements on the emission of greenhouse gases are ineffective?'

Political

- Kyoto Agreement (international)
- USA not a signatory
- Welfare
- Electability

Economic

- Cost benefit
- Developing countries
- Employment
- Demography

Social

- Health
- Employment
- Leisure
- Transport

Technical

- Other energy sources

Environmental

- Ozone depletion in stratosphere
- Greenhouse gases in the troposphere
- Transport

Legal

- Treaties
- Compensation
- Enforcement/sanctions

Using any structured approach to brainstorm the question does not mean you dismiss other ideas and thoughts you may have outside the structure. Any ideas and thoughts from wherever they come are of value and should be considered when finally planning the structure of the essay.

Although scrap paper will not be available during the test you will be provided with a portable whiteboard and pen in your workstation area, specifically for the purpose of planning the essay before typing the final version. Remember, you will have the advantage of being able to edit your essay on-screen.

Plan the structure

Whatever technique you have used to brainstorm your chosen question you should now have sufficient material with which to plan your structure.

Again, although it seems pretty obvious to say so, all essays need a beginning, a middle, and an end but it is surprising how often even good students forget this rule. A useful way to apply the rule is as follows:

- The beginning is the **tell them what you're going to tell them** part of the essay. The opening paragraph or paragraphs gives the reader, in this case an examiner, advance notice of the overall direction and substance of your essay.

- The middle is the **tell them** part of the essay. Tell them the answer to the question which, if using the mnemonic structure, would include the substance of the SWOT or PESTEL analysis.

- The end is the **tell them what you've told them** part of the essay. In this part you can summarise or synthesise your arguments or analysis, that is, succinctly answer the question that has been asked: 'What are the arguments for and against the introduction of proportional representation in general elections?' or 'What is your response to the view that the international agreements on the emission of greenhouse gases are ineffective?'

Write the essay

The most effective way of creating a structure is by the use of paragraphs. There will be a paragraph for the introduction, separate paragraphs for each of the 'arguments' and a paragraph for the conclusion. You are not writing a short story with its discursive narrative; you are providing an analysis of the question and developing reasoned arguments.

The content of the introductory paragraph is very important. It provides the opportunity to grab the attention of the reader. The introduction will reflect how good or bad the rest of the essay is going to be (and how it will be perceived by an examiner who has many more ahead of him or her!). It must set the scene and give a direction as to what can be expected in the body of the essay (not in the conclusion). In this way, the introduction shares similarities to an advocate's opening submission to a court, jury or tribunal: it indicates where the author is going to take them.

In relation to paragraphing the 'arguments', where you are considering 'arguments' and 'counter-arguments', you may prefer to present these opposing views in separate paragraphs.

There is no hard and fast rule about the length of paragraphs though it is suggested that varying their length does make the essay more readable. Whatever, don't get hung up about it and concentrate on the content of the essay not the length of paragraphs.

The structure of a paragraph is not a science but a simple rule of consistency that will make sure you stick to the game plan and not waffle on about irrelevant matters. This rule of consistency is in three parts. Normally the opening part of a paragraph will be where you describe the issue or argument that the paragraph will cover. The second part is where you develop on this issue or argument, providing a better understanding of what you're talking about. The third part is providing the evidence in relation to the issue or argument.

Writing the concluding paragraph should be the easiest part of your essay. What you have stated in your essay can be pulled together in the conclusion, for example, do the pros outweigh the cons? However, it is seen as beneficial if the conclusion is as thought-provoking as possible. This might include discussing the wider implications of the issue, what might happen if the issue remains unresolved, or what you consider could be done to resolve the issue.

One other simple rule is KEEP IT SIMPLE! Think of books you have read where the author appears to be with you and talking to you. Writing is like talking but in print.

When you have thought about what you want to say in your essay, say it as clearly as you can. Keep your sentences as short as possible and read them back to yourself when you've written them to make sure they say what you intended.

Throughout your writing remember, time is of the essence: you only have 30 minutes to write the essay.

Revision

Ideas are organic in that they grow and develop over time. Consequently, at stages throughout your writing other ideas will come to you that have not been included in the structure. You may consider that some of these ideas are sufficiently important to issues or arguments you have raised that it is essential they are included. When you think of them note them down on the whiteboard provided so that you don't forget them. You will have the opportunity to edit your essay and insert any amendments. If this is not possible they can often be inserted within the final section of the essay where you are providing a summary or synthesis of the issues or arguments.

13. Critical thinking

Critical thinking is about how we approach problems, questions and issues. It is suggested by academicians as the best way in which to get at the truth. As already stated earlier in this book, the capacity for critical thought is acknowledged as a valuable intellectual asset in higher education. This part of the chapter only provides a short overview of critical thinking as there are a number of texts readily available.

Critical thinking is not really a new concept to philosophers and scholars and has actually been around for some time in other guises. For example, in his book *The Improvement of the Mind*, published by Gale and Curtis in 1810, Isaac Watts said, 'Though observation and instruction, reading and conversation, may furnish us with many ideas of men and things, yet it is our own meditation and the labour of our own thought that must form our judgement of things. Our own thoughts should join or disjoin these ideas in a proposition for ourselves: it is our mind that must judge for ourselves concerning the agreement or disagreement of ideas, and form propositions of truth out of them. Reading and conversation may acquaint us with many truths and with many arguments to support them, but it is our own study and reasoning that must determine whether these propositions are true, and whether these arguments are just and solid.'

What is critical thinking? Probably the most comprehensive and recent longitudinal study of what constitutes critical thinking was carried out in the United States and Canada. This was a two-year research project involving mainly people in the humanities, sciences, social sciences, and educational field. It was conducted on behalf of the American Philosophical Association and the results were published under the title *Critical Thinking:*

A Statement of Expert Consensus for Purposes of Educational Assessment and Instruction, California Academic Press, Millbrae, CA, 1990.

The research identified a number of core critical thinking skills which include interpretation, analysis, evaluation, inference, explanation and self-regulation, and we will briefly look at each of these skills separately:

Interpretation

This is about comprehension and expression. It is the ability to be able to understand and give meaning to a wide variety of things, such as a problem, situation, event, rules, procedures, etc.

Analysis

To analyse something we break something down into its constituent parts to see what it actually means. It might be examining ideas or looking for arguments such as identifying what is similar or different between approaches to the solution of a problem. It could also be about identifying unstated assumptions in an article or book.

Evaluation

When we evaluate something we are seeking to establish whether something is credible. This could be judging an author's credibility, comparing the pros and cons of alternative interpretations, or judging whether evidence supports a conclusion.

Inference

This is concerned with the skills of deduction and conclusion. It is the ability to consider information in whatever format and draw from it reasonable conclusions. This might include identifying the implications of advocating a particular position on a subject, or even developing a set of options for addressing a particular problem.

Explanation

Explanation is really self-explanatory! It is the ability to be able to explain the results of one's reasoning. For example, when relating the evidence which might have led you to accept or reject a particular position on an issue.

Self-regulation

This is about consciously monitoring what you are doing. For the purposes of the essay it is to be aware of what you are actually writing. You must remain questioning of your biases and personal opinions and assumptions. Really it is a checking mechanism to reconsider your interpretation or judgement to be sure it is focussed on what is required.

The above are considered to be the six cognitive components of critical thinking. A way of encompassing how these skills are used can probably best be demonstrated by considering the effectiveness of solicitors and barristers in our courts. They use reasons to try and convince a judge or jury of a person's guilt or innocence. They evaluate the significance of the evidence presented by the other party and analyse their arguments. They interpret evidence for their client's benefit, make inferences which may or may not be substantiated and give explanation to events or issues. It can be assumed that they are also self-regulating in relation to the protocol required by the court and their own personal biases and beliefs.

Critical thinking is not confined to the cloisters of education but can be characterised by how a person approaches life and living in general. It is something that can be learned and research has shown that there is a significant correlation between critical thinking and reading comprehension. Improvements in critical thinking are paralleled by improvements in reading comprehension.

14. Developing the use of grammar, sentences and punctuation

The purpose of this section is to examine a few of the more important 'rules' of grammar, the construction of sentences and the use of punctuation which might impact on the presentation of your essay. You may have expected to find a section on spelling but this was considered unnecessary. This is not because everyone is good at spelling or that it is unimportant – poor spelling can detract from the contents of an essay and adversely affect the examiner's overall appraisal. The fact is that most of us have a good idea of the words we repeatedly spell incorrectly so maybe we should write these down and practise them. Remember, you will not have the benefit of a 'spell check' function.

Grammar

There is nothing mysterious about grammar except the vocabulary most textbooks use to describe it. It is widely accepted that if you can read, write, speak and think to a reasonable level you should not have a problem with grammar when writing essays. Having said that, it may still be beneficial to consider briefly those 'rules' of grammar relating to the use of sentences. Again, remember that you will only have limited word-processing functions available to you such as 'cut', 'copy' and 'paste', you will not have a 'grammar check' function.

Subject, verb and object

Subject, verb and object is the most common structure of a simple sentence.

The 'subject' of a sentence is what the sentence is about.

The 'verb' is marked for tense and normally matches its subject in person (I, she, they) and number (singular or plural).

The 'object' of a sentence is the person or thing on which the action of the main verb is performed.

An example of the structure of a simple sentence is:

My father (subject) likes (verb) beer (object).

- That said, most sentences will be longer than the simple sentence example and may contain several 'subjects' and 'verbs'.

Main clause and subordinate clause

The 'main clause' is a group of words that contains a subject and a main verb: it is the main structure of the sentence and can stand on its own as a sentence.

The 'subordinate clause' is a group of words that gives further information about the main clause. It may contain a finite or non-finite verb but cannot stand on its own as a sentence.

Simple sentence, compound sentence and complex sentence

A 'simple sentence' consists of a single main clause.

A 'compound sentence' consists of two or more simple sentences joined together by a co-ordinating conjunction such as 'and', 'but' or 'or'.

A 'complex sentence' consists of one or more main clauses and one or more subordinate clauses.

Sentences

Before starting to write your essay it is important to structure what you are going to say. This does not necessarily mean a structure will ensure you can produce a well-written essay but it will give you a good point at which to start.

It is often the case that, due to the candidate's anxiety, the first sentence of an essay is poorly written. Give some thought to the first sentence as it not only gives the examiner a clear picture of what the essay is about but also will have an initial impact on his or her expectations. If you start with low expectations it is unlikely that these will be raised, particularly for the examiner.

Remember the tense of your essay, and try to avoid chopping and changing between first and third person.

It is advisable to start with a simple sentence and then move on to more complicated sentences. The first sentence can simply state the issue being discussed in the paragraph before moving on to greater explanation in the following sentences. In all the sentences, always remember the 'rule' of sentence structure, subject–verb–object.

When you move on to another issue within your essay, always start with a new paragraph. This will tell the examiner that you are raising a different issue even before he or she starts to read the new paragraph. The use of paragraphs also makes the essay look the part as well as being easier to read.

Punctuation

Most writers of books on punctuation suggest that it is important to passing examinations, especially where people are having difficulty with it in writing essays. Well, they would, wouldn't they! This section intends to look briefly at those areas of punctuation where people seem to make most errors; these are the use of full stops and commas.

Full stops

Every student knows that a sentence starts with a capital letter and ends with a full stop. Well, they do until they enter the examination room when this simple rule is often left outside. It is simply the pressure. Breaking the rule consistently throughout your essay will make it difficult for the examiner to easily understand what you're trying to tell him or her. In fact the examiner will probably get to a point of failing the essay without fully reading it. So do remember 'capital letter' and 'full stop' for every sentence.

Commas

Commas can often appear to be randomly spread throughout an essay for no rhyme or reason. As with all punctuation, there are precise rules about the use of commas and each of these 'rules' is described below:

Linking two subject areas in one sentence

Take the following two sentences:

- **I like to go out on a Saturday night. When I do go out I usually visit my local pub.**

It is OK to write two separate sentences like this but they could also be joined together. The linking of sentences can usually be done by using the words 'and', 'but', or 'or' AND the use of a comma. In joining the two sentences mentioned above the word 'and' and a comma would be used, as follows:

- **I like to go out on a Saturday night, and when I do go out I usually visit my local pub.**

The main reason for joining two sentences in this way is to make the essay more readable as it flows better than having to read continuous short sharp sentences.

After an introductory word or phrase
A comma is required where we have used an introductory word or phrase, for example:

- Well, if you want to believe everything you are told.
- Of course, he was always going to get that job.
- Around the world, over half the population live in poverty.

Extending a sentence
We sometimes want to add something to the end of a sentence that would not really sound right by itself, for example:

- **Sex education in schools is a very important part of the syllabus, although some would disagree.**

However, a comma is not always necessary in such cases, which means you would be correct either with or without one!

Using however, therefore, of course, for example, indeed, in fact, nevertheless

These are technically known as parenthetical expressions, but enough of that language. If you use one of these words or phrases at the beginning of a sentence it must be followed by a comma, for example:

- **However, during extra time the home team scored the deciding goal.**

If you use one of these words in a sentence it must be preceded AND followed by a comma, for example:

- **There is, however, more to it than meets the eye.**

Appositives
You know what this is but just can't put your finger on it. It's a noun or phrase that renames another noun just before it, for example:

- **John Duff, Scotland's heaviest man, now weighs over 33 stone.**

This rule is more often used in relation to book titles, for example:

- **Alison Dewart's latest novel, *Hell Hath No Fury*, has been nominated for The Man Booker Prize.**

'Scotland's heaviest man' and '*Hell Hath No Fury*' are the appositives here.

Series of words

This is probably the context of comma use that most people are aware of. It is where the commas are used within a series of words, for example:

- **There is no national hunt racing at Ludlow during June, July, August and September.**

However, probably the best advice on the use of commas is: IF IN DOUBT LEAVE IT OUT.

A final word. There is no doubt that examiners should be more concerned with the content of the essay and not the format, grammar, punctuation and spelling. This may be true but an essay that is pleasing on the eye and easy to read and understand must affect the examiner's approach, even subconsciously. After all, they are only human!